To the Georgies and the Cyndis of the world

who love walks in the rain

who know cookies cure everything

who think chocolate and soda are breakfast foods

who have a new wardrobe if and when they iron

who start the laundry on monday and finish it on sunday

and who believe older really does mean wiser,

this book's for you!

Contents

Introduction

*O*ur spiciest title yet, *Quick Mexican Cooking*, was actually created years ago in Cyndi's kitchen where Mexican food is even prepared for the holidays. It wasn't until we decided to do our *One Foot in the Kitchen* series that the book became a reality, following *Quick Crockery Cooking* to become the second in the series.

Well, things haven't changed much with Cyndi and I. She is still very organized and into making incredible homemade dishes. However, recently she did confess to using canned green chili sauce, but don't tell her I told you. This was probably an isolated lapse on her part since she makes all her Mexican dishes from scratch. So, there is Cyndi outside growing tomatoes and chile peppers and inside cooking refried beans, salsa and green chili sauce. The thing is, the Cyndis of this world are so darn organized they just automatically chop the lettuce while the meat is browning, make a double recipe so there is one in the freezer, and make enough refried beans at one setting to last forever. And, she does it all so efficiently that it takes no time at all.

Me, I'm still the Queen of Easy. I still think quick should be fifteen minutes — three if I can get away with it. I like to think of myself as an "efficient assembler" when it comes to Mexican cooking. Although I prepare my own meats and vegetables, I buy most everything canned, sliced, diced and shredded from the grocery store. It's my way of helping out the economy. This is not to say we don't enjoy good Mexican food at the Patrick's; we do, especially chili. I grew up eating some of the hottest chili in the world, and although my own recipes are mild in comparison, we love them on cold Colorado nights.

The recipes in *Quick Mexican Cooking* are easily adapted to suit both the Georgies and Cyndis out there. If the recipe calls for canned salsa, feel free to choose one of our recipes and make your own. However, if time is of the essence or you're just too tired, don't beat yourself to death when you decide to use that old can.

Georgie

Footnotes from Cyndi and Georgie

Mexican food is fun to cook, tastes good and is easily dressed up with colorful vegetables. Neither of us claim to be experts on Mexican food, but we enjoy cooking and eating it. Like you, our cooking time is limited, but we feel that meal time is an important sharing time of day and want you to enjoy it. We have chosen, adapted and created recipes that are easy to follow with ingredients that should be readily available in grocery stores. Here are some tips to make it all even easier.

- Chile peppers come in many varieties of size, color and heat. Chiles used in recipes in *Quick Mexican Cooking* are primarily canned or fresh green chiles and hotter jalapeño peppers. Feel free to experiment to create a flavor to your taste.

- Preparation and cooking time, in most cases, can be done within an hour. For QUICKer preparation, buy vegetables already diced or chopped, cheese already grated or shredded, and meat already boned and cut into pieces. However, the most economical way is to do it all yourself and buy in quantities when your grocer is having a sale.

- Stock cupboards with most used items like beans, chiles, canned tomatoes and sauces.

- Use a food chopper, processor or blender for QUICKer chopping. Recruit family members or guests to chop vegetables and shred cheese.

- Be efficient and do chopping or extra mixing while waiting for meat to cook.

- Cook more than one meal at a time. It doesn't take much longer to fix extra meat or double a casserole for another meal. Cook beans overnight in a slow cooker (remember to rinse and sort beans carefully).

- Prepare casseroles the night before or early in the morning and bake upon arriving home.

- Fresh vegetables and herbs add special flavor and when in season are more economical. Interchange fresh with canned or frozen ingredients and let creativity shine.

- Lowfat cheese, sour cream and lean meat cut calories and fat without noticeably altering flavor and texture.

Notes:

Starters & Salsas

FROZEN MARGARITAS

What is Mexican food without a Margarita?

1 (12-ounce) can frozen margarita mix
1/2 juice can tequila
Splash triple sec
15 ice cubes
Fresh lime slices, halved
Salt in flat dish

Put all ingredients, except lime and salt, in blender. Whirl on high until blended. With one lime slice, pinch on and move around top of each glass to make wet. Set aside that piece lime. Dip glass in salt. Garnish each glass with slice of lime.
Serves 4.

Per person: 239 calories; 0.2 fat grams

 Make nonalcoholic drinks by eliminating tequila and triple sec and adding 3 cans of water to frozen margarita mix. Salt is always optional.

SANGRIA

Try this hot without the club soda—a great way to warm up after a cold-day adventure.

1/2 cup sugar, optional
1/2 cup orange juice
1 (4- to 5-quart) dry red wine
1/4 cup brandy
1 (7-ounce) bottle club soda, chilled
Apple slices
Orange slices

In pitcher or punch bowl, mix sugar and juice until dissolved. Stir in wine and brandy. Chill until ready to serve. Just before serving, add club soda. Garnish with apple and orange slices. Serves 6.

Per serving: 123 calories; 0 fat grams

 If you want a nonalcoholic Sangria, substitute grape juice for the wine and brandy. Increase the club soda to a 16-ounce bottle.

GUACAMOLE

3 ripe avocados
1/4 cup finely chopped onion
1/4 cup salsa
1 tablespoon lemon juice
Garlic salt to taste
2 tablespoons reduced-fat mayonnaise or
    sour cream

Remove skin and seeds from avocados. Mash with fork. If serving right away, add remaining ingredients and mix. If making ahead, mix together all ingredients except mayonnaise and transfer to serving dish. Spread mayonnaise over top of mixture to prevent browning. Mix together before serving. Serves 8.

Per serving: 107 calories; 10.1 fat grams

 Put on top of a hamburger with melted hot pepper cheese and your favorite condiments.

GEORGIE'S QUICK GUACAMOLE

3 ripe avocados
1 package guacamole mix (found in pro-
    duce section of grocery store)
2 dashes hot pepper sauce
1/4 cup finely chopped onion
1 small tomato, diced

Remove skin and seeds from avocados. Save 1 seed. Dice avocados; mash with fork. Add mix and pepper sauce; stir well. Stir in onion and tomato. Transfer to serving bowl and place seed in the middle of guacamole to prevent browning. Remove seed just before serving. Serves 8.

Per serving: 98 calories; 8.6 fat grams

MEXICAN BEAN DIP

Leftover bean dip is a great spread inside burritos.

1 (8-ounce) package light cream cheese,
    softened
1 (10 1/2-ounce) can bean dip
1/4 teaspoon hot pepper sauce
1 cup light sour cream
1/2 package taco seasoning
1/2 cup chopped green onions
1 cup shredded sharp cheddar cheese
1 cup shredded Monterey Jack cheese

Preheat oven to 350°. Spray deep dish pottery baking dish. Mix all ingredients together, except Jack cheese. Pour into baking dish and top with Jack cheese. Bake 15 minutes. Serve with tortilla chips or crackers. Serves 8.

Per serving: 262 calories; 19.8 fat grams

 Spice this dip up a bit by mixing in a diced jalapeño pepper.

LAKE CHARLES DIP

A friend shared this recipe on a visit from Texas.

3 avocados, mashed
1 cup light sour cream
2 (1-ounce) packages Italian dressing mix
1 tablespoon mayonnaise
1 tomato, diced
Dash hot pepper sauce

Combine all ingredients and serve with tortilla chips. Serves 8.

Per serving: 116 calories; 10.6 fat grams

 Hot pepper sauce is extracted from the tabasco pepper, the only pepper from which a liquid can be extracted.

SEVEN LAYER DIP

Always a QUICK favorite for potlucks.

3 avocados, mashed
2 tablespoons lemon juice
1/2 teaspoon garlic salt
1 cup sour cream
1/2 cup mayonnaise
1 package taco seasoning mix
1 (28-ounce) can jalapeño refried beans
1 cup chopped green onions
1 (6-ounce) can sliced black olives
3 tomatoes, chopped
1 (12-ounce) package shredded cheddar
    cheese

In medium bowl, mix avocados, lemon juice and garlic salt. In separate bowl, combine sour cream, mayonnaise and taco mix. Stir beans and spread in bottom of 12x15-inch serving dish or large platter. Top with avocado mixture. Next, spread on sour cream mixture. Sprinkle with onions, olives, tomatoes and cheese. Serve with tortilla chips. Serves 10.

Per serving: 415 calories; 30.1 fat grams

HEIDI'S BEAN DIP

Easy and delicious.

1 (10-ounce) can refried beans
1 (4-ounce) can green chiles
1/2 cup salsa
1 cup shredded cheddar cheese

In large saucepan, combine all ingredients. Heat through. Transfer to a slow cooker to keep warm. Serve with tortilla or corn chips. Serves 10.

Per serving: 85 calories; 4.5 fat grams

 Spice this one up by using hot Mexican cheese instead of cheddar cheese.

MEXI-CHILE DIP

Try this colorful dip for the holidays. A real favorite, this dip is probably the QUICKest and easiest of all.

1 (8-ounce) package light cream cheese
2 tablespoons mayonnaise
3 to 4 tablespoons milk
1 (4-ounce) can diced green chiles
2 tablespoons finely chopped onion
1 tablespoon pimento
Salt and pepper

Mix cream cheese and mayonnaise together until smooth. Add milk and mix until creamy. Add chiles, onion, pimento, salt and pepper. Refrigerate if not serving right away. Serve with tortilla or corn chips. Serves 6

Per serving: 131 calories; 10.5 fat grams

 Add 1/4 cup green olives and/or 1/4 cup pecan pieces for variety.

QUICK, QUICK CHILE CON QUESO

1 pound light processed American cheese
1 (10-ounce) can chopped tomatoes and
    green chiles
Enough diced jalapeño chiles to taste (to
    Cyndi, the canned tomatoes and
    chiles are hot enough, but some
    like it hotter)

Combine all ingredients. Microwave for 2 minutes and stir. Microwave for another minute and stir. Repeat until cheese is melted. Serve with tortilla chips. Serves 8.

Per serving: 218 calories; 17.8 fat grams

 Use this mixture for a topping on baked potatoes, chimichangas, burritos or tacos.

COLD CHILE CHEESE DIP

This dip is a favorite of Cyndi's husband.

2 cups shredded cheddar cheese
1 cucumber
1 onion
1 (4-ounce) can chopped green chiles
1 medium tomato, chopped
1/4 to 1/2 teaspoon garlic salt

Place cheese into large mixing bowl. In blender or food processor, chop cucumber and onion and add to cheese. Add chiles and tomato to cheese mixture. Lightly toss with fork. Refrigerate until ready to use. Just before serving, add garlic salt. Transfer to chip and dip dish and serve with favorite tortilla chips. Serves 8.

Per serving: 130 calories; 9.6 fat grams

 Try leftover dip in burritos or to top enchiladas.

CHILI-CHEESE DIP

Hearty in character, this dip warms a body after a football game or skiing.

1 pound lean ground beef
1/4 cup chopped onion
1 (8-ounce) can tomato sauce
16 ounces processed American cheese
    with jalapeños, cut in small pieces
1 (4-ounce) can diced green chiles
1 teaspoon Worcestershire sauce
1 teaspoon garlic powder

Brown beef in large skillet; drain. Add onion and cook 5 minutes. Add remaining ingredients, stirring occasionally until cheese melts. Serve warm with corn chips. Serves 12.

Per serving: 252 calories; 19.7 fat grams

 Keep warm in a slow cooker.

CHILE-CREAM CHEESE ROLLUPS

1 (4-ounce) can diced green chiles
1 (8-ounce) package light cream cheese
3 to 4 drops hot pepper sauce
1/2 teaspoon garlic salt
6 soft flour tortillas

Mix chiles, cream cheese, hot sauce and garlic salt together in small mixing bowl. Spread 3 to 4 tablespoons cheese mixture on soft tortilla. Roll up tightly. Repeat until all tortillas are rolled. Slice into 1/4- to 1/2-inch spirals and place on serving dish. Offer salsa for dipping. Serves 12.

Per serving: 103 calories; 4.6 fat grams

 Vary by using red and green peppers and no chiles.

 Try adding a little white cheddar cheese or parmesan cheese to the green chile mixture and heat slightly.

CONFETTI BLACK BEAN DIP

QUICK and best served cold.

1 (15-ounce) can black beans
1/2 cup salsa
2 stalks celery
1 red onion
1/2 green pepper
1/2 red pepper
1 fresh green chile
1 sprig cilantro
1 tomato, finely chopped
Salt and pepper to taste

Drain and rinse beans. Pour into a medium mixing bowl. Add salsa and mix together. Place all other ingredients, except tomato and seasoning in blender or food processor and chop finely. Stir into bean mixture. Stir in tomato, salt and pepper. Refrigerate until ready to serve. Dips well with crackers. Serves 8.

Per serving: 106 calories; 1.1 fat grams

 Substitute black-eyed peas and diced vegetables for a "good luck" New Years dip.

BLACK BEAN DIP

2 (15-ounce) cans black beans, rinsed and
　　drained (divided)
1 1/4 cups salsa, divided
1 cup finely chopped onion
3 cloves garlic, minced
2 teaspoons ground cumin
1/2 teaspoon salt
1/4 cup chopped cilantro, divided
1/2 cup shredded cheddar cheese (can use
　　lowfat)
1/2 cup chopped tomato
1/3 cup light sour cream

Whirl half of the beans and 1/4 cup salsa in food processor or blender until smooth. Sauté onion and garlic in small skillet until onion is tender. Add bean mixture, other half of beans, remaining salsa, cumin and salt. Mix well. Heat to boiling; reduce heat and simmer 10 minutes. Add half of cilantro. Pour into serving dish, top with grated cheese, tomato, remaining cilantro and sour cream. Serve warm with mini tortillas or corn chips. Serves 16.

Per serving: 122 calories; 3.4 fat grams

LAYERED SHRIMP DIP

Georgie's Aunt Sallie has a way of creating spectacular dishes (it runs in the family). This one is directly from Sallie's organized and immaculate kitchen.

1 (15-ounce) can refried beans
1/4 cup salsa
1 cup light sour cream
1 package taco seasoning mix
1 cup shredded cheddar cheese
1 cup chopped lettuce
1 tomato, chopped
3 green onions, sliced
1/2 cup chopped cooked shrimp

Combine beans and salsa. Spread on round platter. Combine sour cream and taco seasoning mix. Spread over bean mixture. Top with cheese, lettuce, tomato, green onion and shrimp. Serve with blue tortilla chips. Serves 10 to 12.

Per serving: 118 calories; 4.7 fat grams

HOMEMADE CORN CHIPS

These are great on a salad, with soups and as a special addition to dips.

1/2 teaspoon chili powder
1/4 teaspoon cumin
1/2 teaspoon garlic salt
1/2 teaspoon parsley
6 lowfat corn tortillas

Preheat oven to 400°. Spray large cookie sheet. In a bowl, mix chili powder, cumin, garlic salt and parsley together. Spray one side of each tortilla with cooking spray and place on cookie sheet. Rub on spice mixture. Bake on top rack 8 to 10 minutes, being careful not to burn, until golden brown. Remove from oven and cut into triangles or strips for serving. Store in tightly covered container. Serves 6.

Per serving: 57 calories; 0.7 fat grams

SUPER NACHOS

Cyndi's family enjoys this as a quick dinner. Sometimes we leave out the ground beef and serve it cold.

1 pound lean ground beef
1 (15-ounce) can refried beans
1 cup light sour cream
1 cup guacamole
6 green onions, chopped
1 (4-ounce) can chopped green chiles
2 cups shredded Monterey Jack cheese
1 cup shredded cheddar cheese
3/4 cup salsa
1 cup shredded lettuce
1 tomato, chopped
1/2 cup sliced black olives
Chips or tortillas

Brown ground beef; drain. Spread beans on large serving platter. Top with ground beef. Layer with remaining ingredients except lettuce, tomatoes and olives. Arrange chips around the outside edges for decoration. Heat in 400° oven 10 minutes (or in microwave 3 minutes). Top with lettuce, tomatoes and olives. Serve with chips or tortillas. Serves 8.

Per serving: 514 calories; 37.6 fat grams

 At Christmas time, layer on a round platter and arrange lettuce, tomatoes and olives around outside to resemble a wreath. For Valentine's Day serve on a heart-shaped platter.

CHILE-CHEESE CUBES

8 eggs
1/2 cup flour
1 teaspoon baking powder
3/4 teaspoon salt
3 cups shredded Monterey Jack cheese
1 1/2 cups cottage cheese
1 (10-ounce) can diced green chiles

Preheat oven to 400°. Spray 9x13-inch baking dish. In large mixing bowl, beat eggs with electric mixer for about 5 minutes. Add flour, baking powder and salt to eggs and mix well. Fold in cheese, cottage cheese and chiles. Pour into baking dish. Bake 40 minutes. Remove from oven and let stand 10 minutes. Cut in small squares; serve hot. Makes 3 to 4 dozen appetizers. Serves 12.

Per serving: 99 calories; 6 fat grams

CHILI HOT WINGS

These wings can be prepared in a slow cooker.

3 pounds chicken, trimmed and cut at
  joints
1 package taco seasoning mix
1/2 cup barbecue sauce
2 tablespoons honey
1 tablespoon soy sauce
1 teaspoon hot pepper sauce
1/2 teaspoon garlic powder

In heavy skillet, mix all ingredients, except chicken. Heat to boiling. Add chicken, stirring to cover. Lower heat and simmer 20 to 30 minutes. Serve with salsa or ranch dressing. Makes about 32 pieces. Serves 8.

Per serving: 148 calories; 3.5 fat grams

 Fresh chiles contain about three times as much vitamin C as oranges, limes and lemons. Some of the more colorful red and yellow chiles have more vitamin A than carrots. All varieties contain vitamin E and potassium.

CHILE-ARTICHOKE DIP

1 (14-ounce) can artichoke hearts, chopped
1 tablespoon minced onion
2 tablespoons diced green chiles
2 tablespoons diced roasted red peppers
1 tablespoon lime juice
Dash of cayenne pepper
Salt to taste
1/2 cup light mayonnaise
Paprika

In medium bowl, mix all ingredients except paprika. Cover and refrigerate until ready to serve. Transfer to serving dish and sprinkle with paprika. Offer thin crackers or tortilla chips. Serves 8.

Per serving: 125 calories; 11 fat grams

 Farmers' markets and roadside stands sell fresh peppers. Buy them roasted and packaged for freezing; use them later in soups, beans, meat and rice.

BEEFY BEAN DIP

1 pound lean ground beef
1/2 cup diced onion
3 teaspoons chili powder
1/2 cup ketchup
1 (15-ounce) can kidney beans, drained and
    rinsed
1 cup processed American cheese with
    jalapeños, diced

In heavy sauce pan, brown beef; drain. Add remaining ingredients; stir constantly over medium heat until cheese is melted. Serve with small flour tortillas or tortilla chips. Serves 12.

Per serving: 267 calories; 11.2 fat grams

Spoon over tortilla chips for hearty nachos.

PARTY CHILE CHEESECAKE

A friend served this at an open house. It was the hit of the party!

1 cup crushed tortilla chips
3 tablespoons butter, melted
2 (8-ounce) packages cream cheese,
    softened
2 eggs
1 (4-ounce) can diced green chiles
1 fresh jalapeño pepper, seeded and diced
1/2 cup shredded mild cheddar cheese
1/2 cup shredded Monterey Jack cheese
1/2 teaspoon garlic salt
1/2 teaspoon cumin
1/4 cup sour cream
Tomatoes, chopped
Green onions, chopped
Black olives, sliced

Preheat oven to 325°. In medium bowl, combine tortilla chips and butter. Press into bottom of 9-inch springform pan (a casserole dish will work). Bake 15 minutes. Meanwhile, in large bowl, blend cream cheese and eggs. Add green chiles, pepper and cheeses. Pour over crust and bake 30 minutes (do not overcook). Remove from oven and cool 5 minutes. Mix garlic salt, cumin and sour cream; spread over top and decorate with tomatoes, green onions and olives. Serve with tortilla chips or crackers. Serves 12.

Per serving: 317 calories; 25.9 fat grams

Cyndi served this recipe with salsa over the top. It added a bit more flavor and heat.

CHILE-CHEESE BALL

1 (8-ounce) package cream cheese, softened
1/2 cup shredded sharp cheddar cheese
1 tablespoon lemon juice
1 to 2 dashes hot pepper sauce
1 teaspoon chili powder
1/2 teaspoon paprika
1/2 cup finely chopped pecans

Mix all ingredients except pecans. Shape into ball or log. Roll in pecans. Serve with crackers. Serves 12.

Per serving: 102 calories; 9.8 fat grams

 This is a great filling for stuffed celery.

CYNDI'S FRESH GARDEN SALSA

This is the salsa I can when my garden produce is at its peak. This recipe makes a small amount, but if you so choose, increase the recipe to accommodate a large pan, pour into pint jars and follow water bath instructions for preserving food.

12 tomatoes, chopped
1 onion, chopped
4 cloves garlic, chopped
4 fresh green chiles, washed, seeded and
    chopped
1/2 teaspoon oregano
1 teaspoon salt (I don't salt too heavily)
1 tablespoon lime juice, lemon juice or
    vinegar
1/2 teaspoon cumin, optional
2 sprigs cilantro, optional

I use the food processor to chop these veggies QUICKly. To vary the recipe, sometimes I add cumin and cilantro. In large saucepan, combine tomatoes, onion, garlic and green chiles. Bring to boil; reduce heat and simmer, uncovered, 10 minutes. Add oregano, salt and juice (plus cumin and cilantro, if desired). Simmer 5 more minutes. Serve with tortilla chips or use in any other recipe that calls for salsa. Makes 4 cups. Serves 16.

Per serving: 25 calories; 0.3 fat grams

 This gets hotter with age.

 If you like a thicker salsa, add 1 (4-ounce) can tomato sauce. Simmer a little longer to thicken salsa.

 HOT TIP

 Foot Note

PORK GREEN CHILI

1 pound trimmed pork steak or pork chops,
    diced (or sausage can be substituted)
1 tablespoon flour
1 tablespoon oil
Salt to taste
Garlic salt to taste
1 (4-ounce) can diced green chiles
1 1/2 cups water (or 1 [15-ounce] can
    tomatoes plus 1/2 cup water)

In large skillet, brown pork with flour in oil. Add remaining ingredients. Simmer 30 minutes to blend. Serves 8.

Per serving: 121 calories; 8.8 fat grams

 Combine small amount of cornstarch and water and slowly stir into hot mixture for a thicker green chili.

COLORADO PORK SALSA

A good friend fixes this recipe which he could never put measurements to, so Cyndi has written it down as remembered. The Duncan family enjoys it as a salsa/gravy over burritos, eggs, etc. or as a spicy chili.

2 cups cubed lean pork (chops or roast),
    trimmed of fat
4 tablespoons flour
3 tablespoons oil
1 large onion, chopped
4 to 6 large cloves garlic, minced
Salt and pepper to taste
2 (15-ounce) cans crushed tomatoes
1 (48-ounce) can tomato juice
1 (7-ounce) can green chiles, coarsely
    chopped

In large pan, cook pork with flour and oil about 10 minutes. Add remaining ingredients. Heat to boiling; reduce heat and simmer 30 minutes, stirring occasionally. Serve over your favorite Mexican dish or on the side as a soup. Serves 20.

Per serving: 82 calories; 5.0 fat grams

 This freezes well and seasons with age.

 Cayenne pepper or red pepper seeds can be added to make salsa spicier.

BLACK BEAN SALSA

Serve cold with tortilla chips or crackers, or serve warm over burritos, tacos or chimis. It's a zesty change.

1 (15-ounce) can black beans, drained
    and rinsed
1 stalk celery
1/2 green pepper
1/2 red onion
2 sprigs fresh cilantro
1/2 (10-ounce) can diced tomatoes and
    green chiles
1/2 teaspoon garlic salt

Pour beans into large mixing bowl. Chop celery, green pepper, onion and cilantro in food processor. Add to beans. Mix in tomatoes with green chiles and garlic salt. Toss gently and transfer to serving dish. Offer tortilla chips or crackers. Serves 8.

Per serving: 92 calories; 0.4 fat grams

GREEN CHILE SALSA

1 (28-ounce) can green chiles
1 onion
2 cups tomatoes, fresh or canned
Garlic salt to taste

Whirl all ingredients together in blender or food processor. Serve hot or cold. Serves 8.

Per serving: 27 calories; 0.2 fat grams

HOT TIP If you don't have a garden, plant chiles in large pots or barrels; at end of the season, pull up plants and dry upside down outside during warm days, bringing them in at night. Use dried chiles throughout the winter.

PICO DE GALLO

3 tomatoes, chopped
1 onion, chopped
1 jalapeño chile, chopped (for milder
    use diced green chiles)
2 sprigs cilantro, chopped
1 teaspoon lemon or lime juice

Combine all ingredients. Serve over any Mexican food dish or with chips, vegetables or crackers. Serves 4.

Per serving: 32 calories; 0.4 fat grams

From experience with her first crop of green chiles and jalapeño peppers, Cyndi found it very important to wear rubber gloves when working with chiles. She had a tingly, burning sensation for three days after preparing those peppers for freezing and not wearing gloves. It's especially important to keep hands away from eyes when working with chile peppers.

ENCHILADA SAUCE

This sauce enhances any Mexican recipe. Homemade is best, but you can buy canned enchilada sauce.

2 heaping tablespoons shortening (you
    can use 3 tablespoons oil)
2 heaping tablespoons flour
2 heaping tablespoons chili powder
1/2 teaspoon garlic salt
2 cups water

Melt shortening on low heat. Add flour, chili powder and garlic salt, stirring constantly (a little browning adds to the flavor). Continue to stir while adding water. It will thicken quickly; add more water if you like it thinner or less water if you prefer a thicker sauce. Serves 4.

Per serving: 83 calories; 7.1 fat grams

 For fewer calories, eliminate flour. Instead, mix 1 1/2 tablespoons corn-starch with 1/4 cup water. Slowly stir into boiling water mixture until thickened.

MEXICAN PESTO

If you like the flavor of cilantro, you will love this "salsa."

3 avocados, cut in pieces
3 cloves garlic
3 tablespoons lemon juice
1/2 cup cilantro
1 teaspoon honey
Salt and pepper to taste

Combine all ingredients, except salt and pepper, in food processor. Whirl until well chopped. Add salt and pepper to taste. Serves 8.

Per serving: 100 calories; 8.6 fat grams

 Serve over your favorite pasta and top with parmesan or a combination of Monterey Jack and cheddar cheese.

PINTO BEAN SALSA

Try this salsa extraordinaire as a dip, side dish or a topping for nachos, grilled meat or burritos.

2 teaspoons oil
1/2 onion, chopped
1 clove garlic, minced
1 jalapeño pepper, chopped
1 (16-ounce) can pinto beans, drained and
    rinsed
1 (16-ounce) can crushed tomatoes
1 teaspoon oregano
1/2 teaspoon cumin
1/2 teaspoon salt
1/2 cup shredded colby-jack cheese

In large skillet, sauté onion, garlic and jalapeño in oil until barely tender. Whirl beans and tomatoes in blender until smooth. Pour into skillet and stir in spices. Simmer to thicken. Transfer to serving dish and top with cheese. Serves 8.

Per serving: 95 calories; 3.6 fat grams

 Generally, small peppers are the hottest, the exception being the Habañero. The larger peppers, like the Anaheim chile, are mild.

MARINARA SALSA

Make Mexican pasta salad in minutes with this salsa.

2 carrots
1 small zucchini
1/2 onion
2 cloves garlic
2 sprigs cilantro
2 teaspoons oil
1 (16-ounce) can Mexican tomatoes
1 teaspoon oregano
Dash of chili powder
1 bay leaf

Chop carrots, zucchini, onion, garlic and cilantro in blender or food processor. Heat oil in large skillet and add chopped vegetables. Sauté 5 minutes. Add tomatoes and remaining ingredients. Simmer 20 to 30 minutes to blend flavors. Remove bay leaf. Serves 6.

Per serving: 44 calories; 1.7 fat grams

It is a tasty warm topping for cooked vegetables or a cold dip for chips or raw vegetables.

CANTALOUPE SALSA

Cyndi loves cantaloupe, so she's always looking for ways to use it!

1 cup cantaloupe, cut into small pieces
3 tablespoons chopped green onion
1 red bell pepper, chopped
3 sprigs cilantro, chopped
1 tablespoon lime juice
Pinch of salt
Pinch of hot pepper flakes

In large bowl, mix ingredients together and chill.
Serves 4.

Per serving: 18 calories; 0.2 fat grams

 This is a nice complement to grilled salmon or your favorite grilled meat.

ZUCCHINI SALSA

Cyndi fixes this salsa often when zucchini are abundant in her garden; it is especially good over omelets and burritos.

2 tablespoons butter
2 cups sliced and quartered zucchini
1 onion, sliced and quartered
1/2 green bell pepper, diced
2 green chiles, diced
1 clove garlic, minced
2 fresh tomatoes, diced
Salt and pepper to taste

In heavy skillet, combine all ingredients and simmer 10 to 15 minutes. Delicious hot or cold. Serves 8.

Per serving: 44 calories; 3.0 fat grams

 Make this really QUICK by whirling all ingredients in blender or food processor, making more of a pesto salsa.

Notes:

Soups

SOUTHWESTERN PASTA SOUP

1 pound lean ground beef
1 medium onion, chopped
2 cloves garlic, minced
1 1/2 teaspoons chili powder
1 teaspoon cumin
3 cups beef broth (or 3 bouillon cubes plus
   3 cups hot water)
2 (10-ounce) cans tomatoes and green
   chiles
1 (4-ounce) can tomato sauce
1 cup uncooked rotini pasta
1 green pepper, chopped
Cheddar cheese, shredded
Tortilla chips

Brown ground beef with onion and garlic in large pan; drain. Sprinkle chili powder and cumin over meat; cook and stir. Add remaining ingredients, except cheese and chips; mix well. Bring to a boil; reduce heat. Cover and simmer about 10 minutes or until pasta is tender. Serve in soup bowls topped with shredded cheese and chips on the side. Serves 8 (one cup servings).

Per serving: 297 calories; 17.8 fat grams

CHICKEN TACO SOUP

1 cooked chicken breast, diced
1 medium onion, chopped
3 cloves garlic, minced
1 (4-ounce) can diced green chiles
2 (15-ounce) cans chicken broth
1 (10-ounce) can enchilada sauce
1 (16-ounce) can crushed tomatoes and
    green chiles
1 (15-ounce) can tomato sauce
1 tablespoon taco seasoning
1 teaspoon chili powder
1 teaspoon cumin
5 corn tortillas, cut into 1/4-inch strips
1 1/2 cups shredded Monterey Jack cheese

In large pan, sauté onion, garlic and chicken 3 to 4 minutes. Add remaining ingredients, except tortillas and cheese. Stir and heat to boiling; reduce heat and simmer 20 minutes. Meanwhile, cut tortillas. Add to soup mixture just before serving. Simmer 5 minutes. Fill individual bowls with soup and sprinkle cheese on each. Serves 8.

Per serving: 289 calories; 15.5 fat grams

CALDO CON QUESO

1 (7-ounce) can whole green chiles
2 1/2 cups water
1 medium tomato, chopped
Garlic salt to taste
1/4 teaspoon pepper
1 (13-ounce) can evaporated milk
1 (10-ounce) can cream of potato soup
1 (10-ounce) can cream of onion soup
8 ounces Monterey Jack cheese, cut into
    small pieces

Rinse, seed and cut chiles into strips. In large saucepan, combine chiles, water, tomato, garlic salt and pepper. Bring to boil. Reduce heat, cover and simmer 5 minutes. Blend in evaporated milk and soups. Put pieces of cheese in soup bowls. Spoon soup into bowls over cheese. Serve with flour tortillas and salad. Serves 4.

Per serving: 408 calories; 27.2 fat grams

CHILE-CHEESE SOUP

1 1/2 cups diced cooked chicken
2 to 3 large potatoes, diced
1 large onion, chopped
1 clove garlic, minced
2 to 3 carrots, sliced thin
3 to 4 stalks celery, sliced thin
1 (4-ounce) can diced green chiles
1 cup corn
2 to 3 chicken bouillon cubes
1 cup water
1 cup processed American cheese, cut
    into small pieces
1/2 cup cream (or milk mixed with 3 table-
    spoons corn starch)
Parsley

Combine all ingredients except cheese, cream and parsley in large pan. Bring to boil; reduce heat and simmer 45 minutes. Add cheese and cream, stirring until cheese has melted. Spoon into bowls. Garnish with parsley. Serve with bread, tortillas or cornbread. Serves 4.

Per serving: 428 calories; 22.6 fat grams

 Use leftover chicken, canned chicken or cook fresh chicken QUICKly in a covered dish in the microwave. Or omit the chicken to make a meatless soup.

GREEN CHILE STEW

This is an unusual dish that will get rave reviews from anyone who tries it.

3 pounds lean boned chuck or round steak
2 (7-ounce) cans diced green chiles
4 onions, chopped
4 tomatoes (or 1 [15-ounce] can)
1 cup water
2 beef bouillon cubes
1 teaspoon salt
2 cloves garlic, minced (2/3 teaspoon garlic
    powder)
1 teaspoon cumin
1/2 teaspoon oregano
1/2 teaspoon chili powder

Brown beef in large pan. Add all other ingredients and simmer 30 minutes to blend the flavors. Serves 6.

Per serving: 369 calories; 11.6 fat grams

 If you prefer a spicier stew, add dried hot pepper flakes.

CREAMY TURKEY CHILI

Great flavor; great change!

4 cups turkey that has been cooked and cut
    into bite-sized pieces
2 carrots, sliced
2 stalks celery, sliced
1 (7-ounce) can diced green chiles
2 (15-ounce) cans white beans
1 (11-ounce) can white corn
3 (14 1/2-ounce) cans chicken or vegetable
    broth, or a mixture of the two
1 (10-ounce) can cream of chicken soup
1 teaspoon oregano
1 teaspoon cumin
1/2 teaspoon white pepper
1 1/2 cups shredded white cheddar cheese
1/2 cup sour cream

Combine all ingredients, except cheese and sour
cream. Bring to boil and simmer 20 minutes. Top
with cheese and dollop of sour cream. Serve with
warm tortillas or corn bread. Serves 10.

Per serving: 467 calories; 16.4 fat grams

Leftover chicken or fish can be substituted for the turkey.

Soups · 53

SAUSAGE AND CHICKEN POT

4 chicken breasts, cubed
1/2 pound chorizo sausage, cut in slices
2 tablespoons oil
2 (10-ounce) cans tomatoes and green
　　chiles
1 (15-ounce) can diced tomatoes
1 (8-ounce) can tomato sauce
1 cup water
1 (15-ounce) can garbanzo beans, drained
1 (15-ounce) can kidney beans, drained
2 sprigs cilantro, chopped
1 teaspoon cumin
1 1/2 teaspoons garlic powder

In large heavy pan, brown chicken and sausage together in oil, stirring often. Drain. Add remaining ingredients and heat to boiling. Reduce heat and cover. Simmer 20 minutes. Serve with warm flour tortillas, cheddar cheese and sour cream. Serves 8 to 10.

Per serving: 405 calories; 15.4 fat grams

 Double this recipe and freeze for a QUICK meal later.

MEATLESS CHEESY CHOWDER

1 cup water
1 chicken bouillon cube
2 potatoes, diced (for QUICK use frozen)
1 (10-ounce) can whole corn
1 red bell pepper, diced
1/4 cup chopped onion
1 cup chopped broccoli
1 teaspoon garlic powder
1/2 teaspoon pepper
1 pound processed American cheese with
 jalapeños
2 cups lowfat milk
Green onions, sliced

In large pan, combine all ingredients except cheese, milk and green onions. Bring to boil and simmer 10 minutes. Meanwhile, microwave cheese and milk on high 2 minutes; stir. Microwave another 2 minutes. Pour into vegetable mixture, stirring constantly to prevent scorching. Heat through and serve garnished with green onion. Serves 4.

Per serving: 582 calories; 38.5 fat grams

 Leftover cooked chicken or turkey makes a good addition to this soup.

TEXAS MEXICAN STEW

2 pounds lean ground beef
1 (28-ounce) can crushed tomatoes
2 cloves garlic, minced
1 (15-ounce) can pinto beans
1 (15-ounce) can kidney beans, rinsed and
    drained
1 (15-ounce) can whole corn, drained
1 cup salsa
1 teaspoon cumin
Salt and pepper to taste

In large pan, brown meat and drain. Add all other ingredients. Simmer 20 minutes without lid, stirring occasionally. Serve with cornbread and whole green onions. Serves 8.

Per serving: 502 calories; 25.5 fat grams

 Leftover roast beef substituted for the ground beef will make this recipe QUICKer.

CYNDI'S FAVORITE CHILI

I like my chili with generous amounts of tomato.

2 pounds lean ground beef or turkey
1 onion, chopped
4 cloves garlic, minced
1/4 cup chili powder
1 teaspoon oregano
1/2 teaspoon cumin
Dash of cayenne pepper
1 (28-ounce) can chili beans
2 (15-ounce) cans crushed tomatoes
1 (15-ounce) can tomato sauce
2 cups water

In large pan, brown meat and drain. Stir in onion, garlic, chili powder, oregano, cumin and cayenne. Cook 5 minutes. Add remaining ingredients and stir together. Bring to boil, reduce heat and simmer 20 minutes. Serve with cornbread or flour tortillas and generous amounts of shredded cheese and chopped onion. Serves 10 to 12.

Per serving: 320 calories; 20.1 fat grams

 HOT TIP Vary this recipe by adjusting the amounts of meat, beans, garlic, or hot peppers.

FAVORITE TEXAS CHILI

There are so many varieties of chili, and most everyone has their own version. The cornmeal makes this one a little different.

3 pounds lean beef stew meat, cubed
2 tablespoons oil
3 cloves garlic, minced
4 to 6 tablespoons chili powder
1 teaspoon salt
2 teaspoons oregano
2 teaspoons cumin
2 teaspoons hot pepper sauce
6 cups water
1/3 cup cornmeal

In heavy pan, brown meat in oil. Add remaining ingredients, except cornmeal. Simmer 45 minutes. Add cornmeal and simmer 15 more minutes. Serve with rice and beans and top with chopped onions. Serves 6 to 8.

Per serving: 673 calories; 45.2 fat grams

FASTEST CHILI IN TOWN

It's a Patrick family favorite, for a quick meal on a chilly night. Georgie serves relishes, pickles, cheese, chopped onion and cinnamon rolls with this chili.

1 pound lean ground beef
1 package chili mix
1 (15-ounce) can tomato sauce
1 (15-ounce) can pork and beans
1 (15-ounce) can water
Shredded cheese, optional for garnish
Chopped onion, optional for garnish

In large saucepan, brown beef; drain. Add remaining ingredients. Simmer over medium heat 15 minutes. Garnish with shredded cheese and chopped onions. Serves 4.

Per serving: 407 calories; 24.7 fat grams

 Serve this recipe over corn chips. Top with lettuce, tomatoes, cheddar cheese and taco sauce.

SOUTHWEST CHILI

A chili that clears the sinuses.

1 1/2 pounds lean ground beef
2 cups chopped onion
3 cloves garlic, minced
4 jalapeño chiles, chopped
1 teaspoon cumin
1/2 teaspoon oregano
1/4 cup chili powder
1 (15-ounce) can beef broth
3/4 cup beer
1 (10-ounce) can tomatoes and green chiles
2 corn tortillas, cut into small strips

In heavy pan, brown beef; drain. Add onion, garlic and jalapeños. Simmer 5 minutes. Stir in cumin, oregano and chili powder. Add broth and beer. Simmer 15 minutes. Stir in tomatoes and tortillas. Simmer 10 more minutes. Serve in soup bowls topped with shredded pepper cheese and a sprig of cilantro. Serves 6.

Per serving: 375 calories; 24.4 fat grams

 HOT TIP Cut some of the heat by substituting a milder chile for the jalapeños.

A HONEY OF A CHILI

1 1/2 pounds lean ground beef
1 large onion, chopped
1 teaspoon garlic salt
1 (28-ounce) can whole tomatoes
1 (8-ounce) can tomato sauce
1 stalk celery, sliced
3 tablespoons chili powder
1 1/2 teaspoons salt
2 tablespoons sugar
1 teaspoon Worcestershire sauce
2 (16-ounce) cans chili beans
1/8 cup honey

In large pan, brown beef with onion and garlic; drain. Stir in remaining ingredients. Heat to boiling and simmer 40 minutes. Just before serving add honey. Stir well. Serves 6.

Per serving: 482 calories; 25.8 fat grams

BEEF AND BLACK BEAN SOUP

1 pound lean ground beef
1 (19-ounce) can black bean soup
1 (15-ounce) can black beans, rinsed and
    drained
1 1/3 cups water
1 cup medium spiced chunky salsa
1/4 cup light sour cream
1/2 cup shredded Monterey Jack cheese
1 cup crushed corn chips
1/4 cup thinly sliced green onions

In heavy pan, brown beef and drain. Stir in soup, black beans, water and salsa. Bring to a boil; reduce heat and simmer, uncovered, 15 minutes. Ladle soup into bowls. Top with sour cream, cheese, chips and green onions. Serve with cornbread and salad. Serves 6.

Per serving: 607 calories; 31.6 fat grams

HAM AND GREEN CHILE CHOWDER

Use leftover Christmas or Easter ham in this recipe. Of course if you're Cyndi; you won't have any left-over ham because she cooks Mexican for the holidays.

2 cups cubed lean ham
1 (7-ounce) can diced green chiles
1 (15-ounce) can whole kernel corn with
    liquid
1 (11-ounce) can creamed corn
2 potatoes, diced
1 carrot, shredded
2 (15-ounce) cans chicken broth
1 (15-ounce) can water and milk, mixed
1 teaspoon oregano
1 teaspoon chipotle spice
1 1/2 cups cubed white cheddar cheese

In large pan, combine all ingredients except cheese. Bring to boil. Reduce heat and simmer 30 minutes, stirring occasionally. Ladle into soup bowls. Stir in 2 to 3 cubes cheese. Garnish with green onion tips. Serve with salad and crackers. Serves 6 to 8.

Per person: 270 calories; 14.2 fat grams

 HOT TIP Chipotle peppers are smoke-dried jalapeño peppers. You can find chipotle spice blends in the spice section of the grocery store or at craft fairs where we found ours.

TORTILLA SOUP

Randi, a co-worker of Cyndi's, came to Cyndi's house and showed her how to put this together. It's fun to do, delicious to eat and it's an authentic, popular soup in Mexico. It sounds complicated but is very easy, especially if you have a helper.

2 chicken breasts
4 (15-ounce) cans chicken broth
2 quarts water
2 teaspoons salt
1 teaspoon garlic powder
1 teaspoon oregano
2 tomatoes, diced
3 green onions, chopped
1 jalapeño pepper, diced
2 sprigs cilantro, chopped
1 tablespoon olive oil
1 tablespoon lemon juice
Salt to taste
1/2 pound white cheddar cheese, cubed
1 to 2 ripe (but firm) avocados, diced
1 onion, diced
1 New Mexico red chile, sliced in strips
3 tablespoons oil
12 corn tortillas, 1-inch strips

In large pan, place chicken breast in chicken broth, water, salt, garlic powder and oregano. Bring to boil, lower heat and simmer 10 to 15 minutes. Remove chicken breasts to a cutting board and shred. Return to chicken broth mixture. While chicken is cooking, prepare pico de gallo by combining tomatoes, onions, jalapeño, cilantro, olive oil, lemon juice and salt. Spoon into serving dish. Prepare cheese, avocados, onion and chile strips in separate dishes. Set on serving table (would work great with a tabletop lazy susan). Just before serving, heat oil in shallow skillet. Add tortillas and cook until firm, not crispy. Add to broth mixture and stir. Serve immediately. Each person adds what they want to the soup. Serves 10 to 12.

Per serving: 368 calories; 21.8 fat grams

 New Mexico red chiles are mild and found in the dried chile/Mexican food section in the grocery store.

POSOLE

Rose, another co-worker of Cyndi's, shared her favorite recipe with us. It is often a traditional Christmas Eve meal. While in Mexico as an exchange student, our friend, Greg, found that everything from the refrigerator was used in posole including anchovies and fruit. He loved it.

2 cups shredded or diced leftover beef or
   chicken
2 (15-ounce) cans hominy
3 cloves garlic, minced
2 large onions, chopped
1/2 teaspoon cumin
1 teaspoon chili powder
1 teaspoon salt
Pepper to taste
4 quarts water

In large pan, combine all ingredients. Bring to boil; lower heat and simmer 30 minutes. Ladle into large soup bowls. Serves 8.

Per serving: 115 calories; 5.0 fat grams

 Hominy is hulled corn with the germ removed and is sometimes used in Mexican dishes.

FISH AND JALAPEÑO CHOWDER

2 teaspoons olive oil
1 onion, chopped
2/3 cup chopped red bell pepper
1/2 cup chopped celery
2 tablespoons chopped pickled jalapeño
    peppers
1 (15-ounce) can white corn
1 (15-ounce) can crushed tomatoes
2 cups frozen potato cubes
1 teaspoon oregano
1/4 teaspoon white pepper
2 chicken bouillon cubes
2 cups water
2 cups fish of choice (cod, salmon, crab or
    shrimp)
1 (12-ounce) can nonfat evaporated milk

In large pan, sauté onion, pepper, celery and jalapeño in oil 5 minutes. Add corn, tomatoes, potatoes, oregano, pepper, bouillon cubes and water. Cover. Bring to boil; reduce heat and simmer 20 minutes. Stir in fish and milk. Heat about 10 minutes (do not over cook). Serves 4.

Per serving: 366 calories; 8.1 fat grams

 If needed, thin soup with a little milk. If you like a thicker soup, stir in 1/4 to 1/2 cup instant potato flakes.

CHICKEN AND GREEN CHILE DUMPLINGS

Some real down-home cooking.

4 cans lowfat chicken broth
1 (15-ounce) can diced tomatoes and
    green chiles
3 cups diced cooked chicken
2 sprigs cilantro, chopped
2 to 3 drops hot pepper sauce
1/2 teaspoon chili powder
1/2 teaspoon cumin
2/3 cup flour
1/2 cup cornmeal
1/4 cup shredded cheddar cheese
1 teaspoon baking powder
Dash of cayenne pepper
1 egg
1/3 cup lowfat milk
1 (4-ounce) can diced green chiles

In large pan, mix broth, tomatoes, chicken and spices together. Bring to boil; lower heat and cover. Simmer while preparing dumplings. Mix together flour, cornmeal, cheese, baking powder and cayenne pepper. In small bowl, slightly beat egg and milk together; stir in green chiles. Pour into flour mixture and stir with fork until moistened. Using a tablespoon, drop dumplings into simmering soup stock. Cover and simmer 20 minutes. Serves 6.

Per serving: 330 calories; 7.0 fat grams

 HOT TIP Substitute a chopped jalapeño in the dumpling mix for a little zest.

TACO SOUP

A friend, Renata, shared this family favorite with us.

2 pounds lean ground beef
1 medium onion, chopped
3 fresh green chiles, chopped (or 1 [7-
    ounce] can diced green chiles)
1 (15-ounce) can lima beans, rinsed and
    drained
1 (15-ounce) can pinto beans, rinsed and
    drained
1 (14 1/2-ounce) can hominy, drained
1 (15-ounce) can red kidney beans, rinsed
    and drained
3 (15-ounce) cans stewed tomatoes
1 1/2 cups water
1 package taco seasoning mix
1 (2-ounce) package ranch-style dressing
    mix
1 teaspoon salt
1 teaspoon pepper

In large pan, brown ground beef; drain. Add remaining ingredients. Simmer 30 minutes. Serve in large soup bowls with shrdded cheese, sour cream and corn chips. Serves 10 to 12.

Per serving: 543 calories; 32.8 fat grams

CHORIZO-CABBAGE SOUP

1/2 pound chorizo, sliced
1 onion, chopped
1/2 cup chopped green pepper
1 (15-ounce) can kidney beans, rinsed and
    drained
1 (15-ounce) can chicken broth
1 (15-ounce) can tomatoes and green chiles
1 cup salsa
2 1/2 cups chopped cabbage
1 teaspoon chili powder

In large pan, combine all ingredients. Bring to boil. Reduce heat; cover and simmer 20 minutes. Uncover and simmer 10 minutes. Top with choice of cheese, white rice or sour cream. Serves 4 to 6.

Per serving: 567 calories; 21.1 fat grams

Notes:

_____
_____
_____
_____
_____
_____
_____
_____
_____
_____
_____
_____
_____
_____
_____
_____
_____
_____
_____

Side Dishes

& Salads

REFRIED BEANS

Beans from scratch are definitely a make-ahead dish. Beans are the greatest (Cyndi's opinion). Add almost anything to them, and they are wonderful.

2 pounds pinto beans, washed (sort
    through for rocks and debris)
Enough water to cover beans by 3 inches
2 tablespoons oil
1 onion, chopped (optional)
1 (4-ounce) can diced green chiles, optional
    (if you prefer hot, add a jalapeño or
    two)
1 teaspoon garlic salt

Cover beans with water and soak overnight. (For QUICK preparations, wash and put in large pan. Add water to cover. Bring to boil and cook 2 to 3 minutes. Remove from heat and allow to set 1 hour.) Rinse. Add oil. Add water to cover by 1 inch. Return to heat and simmer 3 to 4 hours. Add remaining ingredients in last hour of cooking. Extra water can be added during cooking if beans get too dry. Mash with potato masher. Serve in or with your favorite Mexican dish. Serves 20 (based on 1/2 to 3/4 cup servings).

Per serving: 169 calories; 1.9 fat grams

Cooked beans can be frozen and later thawed in the microwave for those QUICK meals.

CONFETTI CORN

2 tablespoons butter
2 (16-ounce) packages frozen corn
1/2 green pepper, chopped
1/2 red pepper, chopped
2 tablespoons chopped onion
Pinch of chili powder

Pour into serving dish and microwave 5 minutes.
Stir. Cook on high another 5 minutes.
Serves 4 to 6.

Per serving: 204 calories; 6.0 fat grams

 This side dish can also be warmed in a saucepan over medium heat.

MEXICAN BEAN CASSEROLE

1/2 pound lean ground beef
1/2 cup finely chopped onion
1/2 teaspoon basil
1/4 teaspoon oregano
1/2 teaspoon salt
1/4 cup diced green chiles
1 (10-ounce) package tortilla chips
2 (15-ounce) cans pinto beans, drained
2 cups shredded cheddar cheese

Preheat oven to 350°. Spray baking dish. In heavy skillet, brown beef; drain. Add onion, basil, oregano, salt and green chiles; cook 5 minutes. Crush 1/3 of the chips and lay on bottom of dish. Spoon half of the beans over chips. Cover beans with 1/2 of meat mixture. Sprinkle 1/2 of cheese over meat mixture. Repeat layers, topping with remaining tortilla chips. Bake 30 minutes. Serves 6.

Per serving: 712 calories; 33.5 fat grams

 This recipe freezes well. Thaw in refrigerator or start heating process in microwave. Increase baking time if cold.

BAKED PINTO BEANS

2 (15-ounce) cans pinto beans, drained
1 cup salsa
1/4 cup ketchup
1/4 cup brown sugar
1 teaspoon cumin
1/2 teaspoon chipotle spice
6 slices cooked bacon, crumbled

In medium saucepan, combine all ingredients. Heat through. Garnish with sliced jalapeños and banana peppers. Serves 6.

Per serving: 308 calories; 5.6 fat grams

Chile powder can be substituted for the chipotle spice.

Banana peppers are found in the pickle section of the grocery store. They are small, yellow and mild chiles.

BEANS AND RICE

A nice complement to grilled fish, chicken or meat. Georgie serves this as a main dish with salad and cornbread.

2 tablespoons butter, divided
1/2 cup chopped green onion
1 cup rice
2 1/2 cups water
1/2 teaspoon salt
1/2 teaspoon cumin
3 stalks celery, sliced
1 onion, sliced and quartered
1 fresh green chile, chopped
1 teaspoon granulated garlic
1 cup chicken broth
2 slices ham, cut in strips (optional)
2 (15-ounce) cans red kidney beans, rinsed
    and drained
1 cup sliced ripe olives (optional)
1/4 cup slivered almonds (optional)
Parsley

In small saucepan, sauté green onion in 1 tablespoon butter about 2 minutes. Add rice, water, salt and cumin. Bring to boil. Reduce heat and simmer 15 to 20 minutes, or until rice is tender and liquid is absorbed. Meanwhile, in another saucepan, sauté celery, onion and green chile in 1 tablespoon butter for about 5 minutes. Add garlic, chicken broth, ham and beans. Heat through. To serve, spoon rice on one side of large shallow soup bowls, then spoon in bean mixture. Top with olives, almonds and parsley. Serves 6 to 8.

Per serving: 319 calories; 8.5 fat grams

Granulated garlic is like garlic salt in appearance without the salty flavor. It's found in the spice section of the grocery store.

CREAMED CORN AND ZUCCHINI

A great way to use zucchini from the garden. Sounds different, but it is yummy!

1 (10-ounce) package frozen corn
2 medium zucchini, sliced
1 onion, chopped
1 clove garlic, minced
1/2 cup lowfat cottage cheese
1/4 cup light sour cream
1 (4-ounce) can diced green chiles
1 teaspoon cumin
Salt and pepper to taste
1 cup shredded cheddar cheese, divided

Preheat oven to 350°. In large mixing bowl, combine all ingredients except 1/2 cup cheese. Stir and pour into casserole dish. Top with remaining 1/2 cup cheese. Bake 30 minutes. Serves 6.

Per serving: 152 calories; 7.2 fat grams

CORN CASSEROLE

Cyndi enjoys this wonderful side dish in restaurants; here is her version for making it at home.

1 egg, slightly beaten
3/4 cup milk
1 (15-ounce) can cream style corn
1 (11-ounce) can whole kernel corn,
    undrained
1 (4-ounce) can diced green chiles
1/3 cup oil
2 tablespoons sugar, optional
1/2 cup shredded cheddar cheese
3/4 cup cornmeal
1/2 teaspoon baking soda
1/2 teaspoon salt

Preheat oven to 400°. Spray 9x9-inch baking dish. In large mixing bowl, combine egg, milk, corn, chiles and oil. Add remaining ingredients, stirring to blend, and pour into prepared baking dish. Bake 30 minutes. Serves 8 to 10

Per serving: 225 calories; 11.6 fat grams

JALAPEÑO CORNBREAD

We moved to Greeley, Colorado about the same time and joined the Newcomers' Club recipe group.
This was a popular recipe which we have both used since.

1 cup butter
3/4 cup sugar
4 eggs
1 (4-ounce) can diced green chiles
1 tablespoon chopped pickled jalapeños
1 (11-ounce) can cream style corn
1/2 cup shredded Monterey Jack cheese
1/2 cup shredded cheddar cheese
1/2 teaspoon salt
1 cup flour
4 teaspoons baking powder
1 cup cornmeal

Preheat oven to 375°. Spray 9x13-inch baking pan. Cream together butter, sugar and eggs. Add remaining ingredients, stirring until mixed (do not beat). Pour into baking pan. Bake 40 to 45 minutes.   Serves 8 to 10.

Per serving: 456 calories; 26.6 fat grams

 For QUICKer baking time use muffin tins. Fill 3/4 full and bake 15 minutes. Check with toothpick to test doneness.

 Add cheese and chiles to a packaged cornbread mix for a QUICK bread.

TRADITIONAL SPANISH RICE

This is the most popular version of Spanish rice.

1/2 cup chopped onion
1 clove garlic, minced
1/2 cup chopped celery
2 tablespoons olive oil or butter
1 cup uncooked rice
1 (4-ounce) can tomato sauce (or 1 cup
    diced tomatoes)
4 ounces (1 can) water
Salt and pepper to taste

Sauté onion, garlic and celery in oil. Add rice and brown slightly. Add remaining ingredients and simmer 15 minutes; check for doneness. Add more water, if necessary. Rice should be tender and liquid should be absorbed. Serves 6.

Per serving: 163 calories; 4.8 fat grams

 Georgie's fool-proof rice: Mix 2 cups of liquid and 1 cup rice, bring to a boil, reduce to simmer, cover and cook 20 minutes. Don't peek!

PEPPER SPANISH RICE

2 tablespoons oil
1 cup rice
4 green onions, chopped
1 (4-ounce) can tomato sauce
1 3/4 cups water
1/4 cup diced red bell pepper
1/4 cup diced green pepper
1 teaspoon salt
1/4 teaspoon garlic powder

In medium saucepan, heat oil. Add rice and onions. Cook 10 minutes until golden brown, stirring often. Stir in remaining ingredients; bring to boil. Reduce heat; cover and simmer 15 to 20 minutes. Add a little more water if rice is dry. Serves 6.

Per serving: 191 calories; 5.0 fat grams

 Use leftover rice in burritos or casseroles.

SPICY SPANISH RICE

Browning the rice adds flavor to this spicier version of Spanish rice.

1 cup rice
2 tablespoons oil
1 onion, chopped
1 clove garlic, minced
2 fresh tomatoes, chopped
1 (4-ounce) can diced green chiles
2 cups beef broth (2 beef bouillon cubes
    dissolved in 2 cups hot water)
1 teaspoon chili powder
1/2 teaspoon salt, optional

In heavy saucepan, brown rice in oil. Add onions, garlic, tomatoes and chiles. Sauté 5 minutes. Add beef broth, chili powder and salt. Simmer 15 minutes, or until rice is tender and liquid is absorbed. Serves 6.

Per serving: 197 calories; 5.89 fat grams

Add 2 to 3 slices bacon and a little cheddar cheese to vary this recipe.

MEXICAN MACARONI AND CHEESE

A new twist to an old favorite.

1 pound uncooked elbow macaroni
1/4 cup olive oil
4 tomatoes, diced (or 1 [15-ounce] can
    diced tomatoes)
2 onions, chopped
1 (7-ounce) can green chiles (or 7 to 8 fresh
    green chiles, diced)
2 (14-ounce) cans beef broth
1/2 teaspoon chili powder
1/2 teaspoon salt
2 cups shredded cheddar cheese

In large heavy skillet, brown macaroni in oil. Add tomatoes, onions and green chiles. Sauté 2 to 3 minutes. Add beef broth, chili powder and salt. Simmer 15 minutes until all liquid has been absorbed. Serve with generous amounts of cheese on top. Serves 6 to 8.

Per serving: 489 calories; 20.6 fat grams

SIESTA POTATOES

Great as a side dish or as a "crust" for an egg dish.

2 tablespoons butter or oil
2 pounds frozen hash browns
1/2 cup cream (can use lowfat milk or
    evaporated milk)
1 (10-ounce) can diced tomatoes and
    green chiles
4 green onions, cut in 1-inch lengths
1 sprig fresh cilantro, chopped (or 1/2
    teaspoon dried cilantro)
1/4 teaspoon oregano
1/4 teaspoon cumin
1/2 teaspoon garlic salt
1/2 teaspoon pepper
1/2 cup shredded hot pepper cheese

In heavy skillet, brown hash browns in butter. Stir in remaining ingredients, except cheese, stirring to keep from sticking and burning. Top with cheese just in time to melt before serving. Serves 8.

Per serving: 129 calories; 9.1 fat grams

MEXI-TATERS

Oh, my, there are so many ways you can create taters! This is just one of them.

4 large baking potatoes
2 cups salsa
2 cups shredded cheddar cheese
1/4 cup sliced olives
1/2 cup light sour cream
2 green onions, sliced

Wash and pierce potatoes with fork. "Bake" in microwave on high 10 to 12 minutes, rotating at six minutes. Split potatoes and pinch to open. Top each potato with salsa, cheese, olives, sour cream and onions. Serve immediately with salad and steamed vegetables. Serves 4.

Per serving: 414 calories; 25.3 fat grams

 Make these taters a main meal by smothering with red or green chili.

 If you like crispy skins, bake in oven at 400° for 1 hour, or after microwaving, bake in oven 10 minutes.

SANTA FE POTATO STUFFED PEPPERS

Stop the presses! This was the recipe that put us behind schedule. Mary, a friend in Steamboat Springs, Colorado, served us a version of this spicy yet elegant side dish. We had to include it here.

2 large baking potatoes, scrubbed clean
1/4 cup milk
1/2 cup shredded sharp cheddar cheese, divided
1/4 cup butter
1/4 cup hot salsa
Salt and fresh ground pepper to taste
4 to 6 whole green chiles (fresh roasted or canned)

Preheat oven to 350°. Spray 9x13-inch baking dish. Microwave potatoes 10 minutes turning after 5 minutes (potatoes should be soft to the touch). Using an oven mitt, slice potatoes in half. Scoop out potato middles into large mixing bowl saving skins for later. Whip potatoes, milk, 1/4 cup cheese and butter until fluffy. Stir in salsa, salt and pepper. Wash, remove seeds and pat chiles dry. Make lengthwise slice in chiles and place in baking dish. With a spoon or a decorator bag fill chiles with potato mixture. Top each with remaining cheese. Bake 10 minutes until cheese is melted and potatoes are heated through. Garnish with reserved skins filled with your favorite Mexican toppings. Serves 4 to 6.

 Mary uses "Religious Experience" brand hot sauce (manufactured in Grand Junction, Colorado). Any hot sauce will work, but this one has a very distinct and recommended flavor.

SKILLET POTATOES

These are great with breakfast, lunch or dinner.

4 cups cubed cooked potatoes
1 tablespoon oil
1 (10-ounce) can cheddar cheese soup
1/2 cup salsa
1 teaspoon granulated garlic

In large skillet, warm potatoes in oil. Add soup, salsa and garlic. Stir often to keep from sticking and scorching. Serves 6 to 8.

Per serving: 243 calories; 16.2 fat grams

MEXICAN VEGETABLES

1 medium onion, diced
1 tablespoon butter
1 medium zucchini, quartered and sliced
1 (15-ounce) can whole kernel corn,
    drained
2 medium tomatoes, cut in wedges
1/4 cup vinegar
1/4 teaspoon salt
1/4 teaspoon chili powder

In heavy skillet, sauté onion in butter; add zucchini. Cook, covered, over medium heat until tender. Add corn and tomatoes. Heat until warm. Meanwhile, in small saucepan bring vinegar, salt and chili powder to boil. Pour over vegetable mixture and toss. Serve as a side dish to your favorite grilled meat. Serves 6.

Per serving: 77 calories; 2.4 fat grams

TACO SALAD

A favorite and easy luncheon or main dish salad. Always a hit at a potluck since there are so many individual variations to this salad.

1 pound lean ground beef
1 onion, chopped (optional)
2 cloves garlic, minced (or 1 teaspoon
    garlic salt)
2 teaspoons chili powder
1/2 teaspoon oregano
1/2 cup salsa
Salt and pepper to taste
1 head iceberg lettuce, torn into bite-sized
    pieces
1 cup shredded cheddar cheese
4 green onions, chopped
1 avocado, sliced (optional)
1/2 cup sliced black olives, optional
3 cups broken tortilla chips
2 tomatoes, wedged

In heavy skillet, brown and drain ground beef. Add onion, garlic, chili powder, oregano, salsa, salt and pepper. Simmer 5 minutes. While meat is browning, break lettuce into large salad bowl. Add cheese, green onions, avocado and black olives. Add meat and toss together. Just before serving stir in tortilla chips. Garnish with tomatoes. Serves 8 to 10.

Per serving: 644 calories; 39.2 fat grams

Red kidney beans can be added.

Omit the avocado in the body of the salad and make a dressing by mashing the avocado and mixing with 2 teaspoons lemon juice and 1/2 cup sour cream.

Toss with Thousand Island dressing.

GEORGIE'S MEXICAN CHEF SALAD

This is a long-time favorite of the Patricks—Georgie's answer to "what's for dinner."

1 pound lean ground beef
1 package taco seasoning mix
1 cup red kidney beans, rinsed and
    drained (optional)
1 head lettuce, torn in pieces
2 tomatoes, chopped
1 onion, chopped
1/2 cup shredded cheddar cheese
1 (8-ounce) bottle Thousand Island dressing
1 avocado, diced (optional)
1 (11-ounce) bag tortilla chips, crushed

In heavy skillet, brown beef; drain. Add taco seasoning and beans; warm. In a large bowl, combine lettuce, tomatoes, onion and cheese. Add meat mixture and dressing; toss. Add avocado and chips; gently toss. Serves 6.

Per serving: 433 calories; 33.9 fat grams

If using flavored tortilla chips, reduce taco seasoning to 1/2 package.

CHICKEN TACO SALAD

Grilling the chicken adds a delightful aroma and flavor to this salad. The chicken can be from a previous meal and served cold.

3 hard cooked eggs
2 chicken breasts
2 tablespoons butter, melted
1 teaspoon chili powder
1/2 teaspoon cumin
6 slices bacon, cooked until crisp
2 cups bite-size spinach leaves
1 head iceberg lettuce, broken into bite-sized pieces
1/2 yellow pepper, thinly sliced
1 small red onion, thinly sliced
1 (15-ounce) can black beans, drained and rinsed
3 cups broken tortilla chips
1 tomato, wedged
Salsa

Cook eggs; run cold water over them until cooled; peel and chop. Start charcoal grill. Mix melted butter, chili powder and cumin in small bowl. Brush chicken with mixture periodically while grilling. Meanwhile, microwave bacon between layers of paper towels on a paper plate about 5 to 6 minutes until crisp. Cool and break. In large salad bowl, toss spinach, lettuce, pepper, onion, beans, eggs, tortilla chips and bacon together. When chicken is done, slice into thin pieces and arrange around the top. Garnish with tomato. Pass the salsa for dressing. Serves 8 to 10.

Per serving: 626 calories; 29.1 fat grams

 Try this one with grilled shrimp.

SOUTHWEST COLESLAW

1 (15-ounce) can black-eyed peas, drained
   and rinsed
1 (11-ounce) can corn, drained
1/2 cup salsa
1 1/2 teaspoons olive oil
1/2 teaspoon red pepper sauce
Salt and pepper to taste
1 clove garlic
2/3 cup chopped green onions
2/3 cup chopped fresh cilantro
2 cups chopped tomatoes
1 avocado, diced
3 cups grated cabbage

Combine peas, corn, salsa, oil, pepper sauce, salt and pepper in mixing bowl. Chop garlic, onions, and cilantro in blender or food processor. Add to vegetables with remaining ingredients. Toss gently. Serves 8 to 10.

Per serving: 131 calories; 4.4 fat grams

 Omit the cabbage and serve this dish as an appetizer with tortilla chips.

STUFFED GREEN CHILES SALAD

2 avocados, mashed
1 tablespoon lemon or lime juice
1/4 teaspoon salt
1/4 teaspoon pepper
1/4 teaspoon chili powder
1 tablespoon grated onion
2 (6-ounce) cans whole green chiles, rinsed
    and drained
Lettuce, shredded
Tomato wedges
Sour cream
Paprika

Combine avocados, juice, salt, pepper, chili powder and onion. Mix well. Slice chiles in half lengthwise Stuff each chile with avocado mixture. Serve 1 or 2 stuffed chiles on lettuce with tomato wedges and a dollop of sour cream sprinkled with paprika. Serves 6 to 8.

Per serving: 155 calories; 8.0 fat grams

THREE-BEAN, THREE-PEPPER SALAD

A creative twist to a traditional recipe.

1 (15-ounce) can pinto beans, rinsed and
    drained
1 (15-ounce) can black beans, rinsed and
    drained
1 (15-ounce) can garbanzo beans, rinsed
    and drained
1/4 cup diced roasted red peppers
2 tablespoons chopped pickled jalapeño
    pepper
1/2 green pepper, chopped
4 green onions, chopped
1/3 cup vinegar
1/4 cup oil
1/4 teaspoon garlic powder
1/4 teaspoon pepper
1/2 teaspoon salt
1/2 teaspoon chipotle spice

Place the first seven ingredients in large bowl. Mix vinegar, oil, garlic powder, pepper, salt and chipotle spice together in small bowl. Pour over bean mixture. Cover and refrigerate until ready to serve. Serves 10 to 12.

Per serving: 557 calories; 9.1 fat grams

 Meaty peppers like cherry, banana and jalapeño are often pickled; they can be found in the pickle section or the Mexican food section of the grocery store.

MEXICAN SALAD

A good friend, Judy, used to serve this dish at big gatherings. It has always been a favorite of the Duncan family, either as an hors d'oeuvre or main dish salad.

2 pounds lean ground beef
3 tablespoons cumin
1 cup chopped celery
1/2 cup chopped red onion
1 cup chopped green pepper
4 cloves garlic, chopped
1 pound light processed American cheese
2 tomatoes, diced
1 (10-ounce) can tomatoes and green chiles
1 head lettuce, shredded
2 cups crushed corn chips
6 to 8 small flour tortillas

In large skillet, brown meat and drain. Add cumin and all vegetables, except lettuce and tomatoes. Meanwhile, cube cheese into medium bowl and add tomatoes and green chiles. Cover and microwave on high 2 minutes. Stir and microwave 2 more minutes or until cheese is melted. Pour into meat mixture. Just before serving, stir in lettuce and chips. Spoon onto tortilla and fold. Serve with extra lettuce and salsa. Serves 8.

Per serving: 984 calories; 64.2 fat grams

 Leftovers make a good enchilada filling, a hearty dip or a topping for poached or fried eggs.

Notes:

Main Dishes

HUEVOS RANCHEROS

Translates as "Ranch Country Eggs." Easy and delicious!!

4 large flour tortillas
1 (15-ounce) can refried beans (or 2 cups
    of your own homemade beans)
1 (15-ounce) can green chili with pork (or
    make your own)
2 cups grated cheddar cheese
4 to 8 eggs (depending on how many each
    person wants)
2 tablespoons butter
Salsa

Lay each tortilla on dinner plate. Spread each with equal amounts of refried beans. Pour equal amounts of green chili over the top and spread 1/2 cup cheese on each. Cover with plastic wrap and microwave on high 1 minute or until cheese melts. While microwaving, fry eggs in butter to order. Place egg(s) on top. Spoon a tablespoon or two of salsa on top of egg. Serve hot with orange slices and/or pan-fried hash browned potatoes. Serves 4.

Per serving: 583 calories; 35.3 fat grams

BREAKFAST BURRITOS

Make extras to put in the freezer for other meals. Take them camping, to sporting events or to eat on the way to work.

1 (2-pound) bag frozen potatoes (hash
    browns, cubes or make your own
    boiled potatoes and chop them)
Salt and pepper to taste
1/2 teaspoon cayenne pepper
8 to 10 strips of bacon, cooked very crisp,
    broken in small pieces
1 cup refried beans
1 onion, chopped
1 (7-ounce) can diced green chiles
1 tablespoon butter
8 eggs, beaten
1 cup salsa
1 cup grated cheddar, Monterey Jack or
    combination of cheeses
1/2 teaspoon salt
1/2 teaspoon pepper
12 flour tortillas, warmed between two
    damp paper towels 30 seconds
    on high in microwave

Pour potatoes into large mixing bowl. Add salt and peppers. Mix in bacon and beans. Set aside. Sauté onion and green chiles in butter. Add eggs and scramble. Add egg mixture, salsa and cheese to potato mixture. Salt and pepper. Toss together and fill tortillas with two heaping mixing spoonfuls. Fold over one edge. Tuck in one end and fold over the other edge. Leave top open for adding extra salsa. Serve hot. To freeze, wrap each in plastic wrap and put in freezer bag. Take out as needed and microwave on defrost until thawed, then on high for 1 minute. (Microwaving too long will make ends of tortilla tough). Serves 12.

Per serving: 405 calories; 22.3 fat grams

 Substitute ham cubes or cooked sausage for bacon or leave out meat and add more beans.

MEXICAN QUICHE

Heidi, Cyndi's daughter, shared this recipe with us.

12 ounces link sausage (can use chorizo)
10 corn tortillas
3/4 cup shredded Monterey Jack cheese
3/4 cup shredded cheddar cheese
2 ounces diced green chiles
1 tomato, chopped
3 eggs, beaten
3/4 cup milk
1 teaspoon chili powder
1 teaspoon salt
1 avocado, optional

Preheat oven to 400°. Spray 9-inch pie plate. Cook sausage and set aside. Place 9 tortillas in pie plate overlapping edges, allowing edges to extend over plate. Place remaining tortilla in center of plate. Combine sausage and cheeses; arrange over tortillas. Cover with chiles and tomato. Beat eggs, milk, chili powder and salt. Pour over meat and cheese mixture. Bake 35 minutes. Remove from oven and let set 5 minutes. Cut into serving portions. Garnish with avocado slices. Serve with fruit, potatoes and salsa. Serves 6.

Per person: 493 calories; 35.7 fat grams

 For QUICKer, microwave on high 4 to 5 minutes to start cooking process. Bake 20 minutes and check.

EASY MEXICAN BREAKFAST PIE

Georgie serves this tasty pie at brunch with salad and fresh fruit.

1 unbaked pie crust
1 medium onion, sliced into strips
1 (4-ounce) can green chiles
1 cup shredded Monterey Jack cheese
1 tablespoon flour
3 eggs
1 cup half and half
1 teaspoon salt
1 teaspoon pepper
1/2 teaspoon chili powder
1/4 teaspoon dry mustard

Preheat oven to 375°. Place onions and chiles on bottom of pie crust. In small bowl, coat cheese with flour. Sprinkle over onion and chiles. In medium bowl, beat eggs; add remaining ingredients and mix well. Pour over cheese. Bake 40 to 45 minutes, or until knife comes out clean. Garnish with a whole pepper and parsley. Serves 6.

Per serving: 304 calories; 20.7 fat grams

 To make this QUICKer, prepare individual quiches by shaping a small flour tortilla in six custard dishes. Prepare as above and divide egg mixture evenly. Check after 20 minutes.

LAYERED BREAKFAST

This is a good casserole to make ahead for a crowd.

1 (2-pound) package frozen hash brown
    potatoes, thawed
1 (4-ounce) can diced green chiles
1 onion, chopped
Salt and pepper to taste
1 1/2 cups grated white cheddar cheese
1 1/2 cups grated mild cheddar cheese
2 (15-ounce) cans refried beans (or use
    your own homemade refritos)
12 eggs, beaten
1 cup low-fat milk
1 teaspoon salt
1/2 teaspoon pepper
1/2 teaspoon oregano
1/4 teaspoon cumin
1/2 cup salsa

Preheat oven to 400°. Spray 11x14-inch baking dish. Toss hash browns, chiles, onion, salt and pepper in large bowl. Transfer to baking dish. In same mixing bowl, combine cheeses. Cover hash brown mixture with 1 cup cheese. Spoon beans over top of cheese. Spread another cup of cheese over the beans. Beat eggs with milk, salt, pepper, oregano and cumin. Pour over beans. Top with remaining cup of cheese. Drizzle salsa over top of cheese. Bake 30 minutes. Serves 8.

Per serving: 737 calories; 41.2 fat grams

Microwave on high 5 minutes to start cooking process.

LIGHT ZUCCHINI SALSA SCRAMBLE

A great way to use fresh produce from the garden.

2 large green chiles (or 1 [4-ounce] can
    diced green chiles)
3 fresh tomatoes (or 1 [15-ounce] can diced
    tomatoes)
1 small onion
2 cloves garlic
2 small zucchinis, quartered and sliced
1/2 teaspoon oregano
Salt and pepper to taste
8 eggs, beaten
Salt and pepper to taste
2 tablespoons butter
1 cup cheddar cheese

Whirl chiles, tomatoes, onion and garlic in blender. Combine with zucchini in medium saucepan. Season with oregano, salt and pepper. Simmer while eggs are being prepared. Scramble eggs in medium fry pan with salt, pepper and butter. Divide eggs on warm plates. Spoon salsa over eggs and top with cheese. Serve with hash browned potatoes, fruit, rice or beans on the side. Serves 6.

Per serving: 223 calories; 16 fat grams

Foot Note

This is a good "breakfast for dinner" dish.

GREEN CHILE FRITTATA

Be creative with this QUICK egg dish. Fresh vegetables, cooked potatoes or leftover meats make a delicious addition.

1 tablespoon butter
1/2 onion, chopped
1 clove garlic, minced
1 cup thawed and chopped frozen broccoli
1 (4-ounce) can diced green chiles
1 tomato, diced
Salt and pepper to taste
8 eggs
1/2 cup lowfat cottage cheese
1/2 teaspoon oregano
Salt and pepper to taste
Salsa
Light sour cream

Preheat oven to 350°. In ovenproof, non-stick skillet, sauté onion, garlic and broccoli in butter 3-4 minutes. Add chiles, tomato, salt and pepper. Whip eggs, cottage cheese and oregano together. Add salt and pepper. Pour eggs over chile mixture and stir to blend. Cook 3 to 5 minutes. Bake until eggs are set, about 15 minutes. Remove; cut into 4 sections. Drizzle 2 tablespoons salsa on top with dollop of sour cream. Serves 4.

Per serving: 221 calories; 13.7 fat grams

BASIC GROUND BEEF FOR MEXICAN DISHES

Use in tacos, tostadas, burritos, enchiladas, chimis, salads and casseroles. Spice to your preference.

1 1/2 pounds lean ground beef
1 onion, chopped
2 cloves garlic, minced
1/2 teaspoon salt
1/2 teaspoon pepper
1/2 teaspoon oregano
1/4 teaspoon cumin
1/2 cup salsa

In heavy skillet, brown ground beef; drain. Add onion and garlic; stir together and cook 5 minutes. Add remaining ingredients and simmer until ready to use in your favorite dish. Serves 6.

Per serving: 316 calories; 24.3 fat grams

 Add your favorite chiles and/or vegetables to use in other dishes.

 Double or triple this recipe, divide into freezer dishes and freeze for a QUICK meal at a later time.

BASIC COOKED CHICKEN FOR MEXICAN FOOD

This is a good make-ahead recipe. You can use any part of the chicken, but we prefer using chicken breasts.

2 chicken breasts, cut in half
1 cup water
1 chicken flavored bouillon cube
1 bay leaf
1/2 teaspoon granulated garlic
Pinch of cumin

Wash and trim chicken pieces. In saucepan, combine all ingredients. Bring to boil; lower heat and simmer 15 to 20 minutes, until chicken is done. Remove chicken pieces and cool. Save broth for soup. Shred or dice chicken for specific recipe. Serves 4.

Per serving: 128 calories; 1.5 fat grams

Use chicken in tacos, burritos, tostadas, chimis, salads and casseroles.

While you are at it, double or triple the recipe for future QUICK meals. It freezes well for about 60 days.

MARINATED PORK

Called "Carne Adovada" by Indians who used the chile pulp to preserve meat before refrigeration was invented. Use this meat in burritos, tacos, enchiladas, salads or breakfast dishes.

1/4 cup chili powder
2 to 3 cups water
4 cloves garlic, minced
1 tablespoon oregano
2 teaspoons cumin
1/4 cup wine vinegar
2 to 3 pounds lean pork tenderloin, trimmed
    of fat and cut into 1 x 1/2-inch strips

Combine all ingredients, except pork, to make a thick marinade. Pour over pork and marinate at least 24 hours. Drain and bake pork at 325° for 1 hour or until tender and done. Serves 4 to 6.

Per serving: 302 calories; 9.0 fat grams

This is a great make-ahead recipe to have in the freezer for an extra fast meal.

MEXICAN BRISKET

If you want this done when you get home at night, put it in your slow cooker in the morning. The preparation time for this brisket is QUICK but would qualify for a make-ahead recipe.

3 pounds boneless beef brisket, trimmed
   of fat
2 tablespoons oil
2 cups mild salsa
3/4 cup water
2 tablespoons white vinegar
1 teaspoon garlic powder
1/2 teaspoon salt
1/4 teaspoon cinnamon
1/4 teaspoon oregano
1/4 teaspoon thyme
1/8 teaspoon cloves
1/8 teaspoon pepper

Preheat oven to 250°. In heavy pan, brown brisket in oil. Combine remaining ingredients and pour over brisket. Bake, covered, 6 hours. Remove to platter, slice thinly across grain. Serve with salsa mixture, Spanish rice or baked potato, and corn. Serves 10 to 12.

Per serving: 430 calories; 37.1 fat grams

SPICY BEEF TO GRILL

Keep the kitchen cool in the summer with this fine meat dish.

1 (3-pound) roast, or 6 (8-ounce) steaks
1 tablespoon chili powder
1/2 teaspoon cumin
1/2 teaspoon salt
1/2 teaspoon cayenne pepper
1 teaspoon coarsely ground pepper

Clean and turn on grill. Trim fat from meat. Mix and rub spices into roast or steaks. Grill 20 to 35 minutes depending on desired doneness, turning occasionally. Top each serving with warm black bean salsa. Serve with vegetable kabobs, salad and warm tortillas. Serves 6.

Per serving: 319 calories; 11.4 fat grams

QUICK BURRITOS BUFFET

An easy way to welcome a crowd.

1 pound lean ground beef
1/2 packet burrito seasoning mix
1 (15-ounce) can refried beans with
　　jalapeños
1 (15-ounce) can pork green chili sauce
 6 flour tortillas
1/2 pound shredded cheddar cheese
1 medium onion, chopped
2 cups shredded lettuce
2 medium tomatoes, chopped

In heavy skillet, brown ground beef; drain. Add burrito seasoning and mix well. In separate dishes, heat beans and green chili in microwave. Warm tortillas between damp paper towels in microwave about 30 to 40 seconds. Set out all ingredients in separate dishes. Offer salsa and tortilla chips. Serves 6.

Per serving: 782 calories; 37.7 fat grams

 Include taco and tostada shells with your buffet for variety.

CHIMICHANGAS

This version of a family favorite is baked, not deep fried, so the mess is nominal.

1 pound ground pork, beef or shredded
    chicken
1 medium onion, chopped
1 clove garlic, minced
3/4 cup salsa
1 teaspoon cumin
1/2 teaspoon oregano
1/2 teaspoon salt
6 flour tortillas
1/4 cup butter, melted
Sour cream, optional
Guacamole, optional

Preheat oven to 475°. Spray 13x9-inch baking dish. Brown meat with onion and garlic; drain. Stir in salsa, cumin, oregano and salt; simmer 5 minutes or until most of the liquid has evaporated. Spoon heaping 1/3 cup meat mixture onto center of tortilla. Fold 2 sides over filling; fold ends down. Place seam side down in baking dish, and brush tops with melted butter. Bake 13 minutes or until golden brown. Top with sour cream and guacamole, if desired. Serve with additional salsa and a side of shredded lettuce. Serves 6.

Per serving: 419 calories; 28.7 fat grams

 Chimis freeze well and heat up nicely in the microwave. For a crispier chimi, remove from microwave and bake in a preheated 350° oven for about 5 minutes.

TACO BURRADAS

These delectables are a combination of tacos, burritos and enchiladas. Your family and friends will think they are heavenly!

1 1/2 pounds lean ground beef (can mix
    half sausage and half beef)
1/2 cup chopped onion, optional
1 1/2 cups salsa or green chili
1 cup refried beans (can be served
    on the side)
1/2 teaspoon cumin
1/2 teaspoon chili powder
1/2 teaspoon oregano
1/4 teaspoon cayenne pepper, optional
Salt and pepper to taste
1 1/2 cups lettuce
8 flour tortillas
2 (10-ounce) cans enchilada sauce
1/2 pound cheddar cheese, shredded

Preheat oven to 350°, or use microwave. Brown meat; drain. Add chopped onion, salsa, beans and spices; simmer 10 minutes. Add lettuce to meat mixture and toss. Spray cookie sheet or casserole dish (if you prefer, you can prepare these right on individual plates and heat in the microwave). Heat enchilada sauce or make your own. Dip tortilla in enchilada sauce and lay in baking dish; fill with meat mixture and roll. Repeat with each tortilla. Top with sauce and cheese. Bake 20 minutes or until hot; or microwave 2 minutes. Serve with more sauce, cheese, sour cream and lettuce. Serves 8.

Per serving: 581 calories; 38.1 fat grams

ENCHILADA PIE

Double the recipe and freeze. This is a popular dish to take to potlucks or friends.

10 corn tortillas (or use tortilla chips)
2 pounds ground beef
1 medium clove garlic, minced (can use
      garlic powder)
1 medium onion, chopped, optional
1 (7-ounce) can diced green chiles
1 (10-ounce) can cream of mushroom soup
1 (15-ounce) can stewed tomatoes
1/2 teaspoon chili powder
Salt and pepper to taste
3 cups grated cheddar cheese

Preheat oven to 350°. Spray 9x13-inch baking dish. Brown meat; drain. Add garlic and onion. Add chiles, soup and tomatoes. Season with chili powder, salt and pepper. Simmer mixture 10 minutes. Tear tortillas and lay in bottom of baking pan. Spoon half of meat mixture over tortilla pieces and sprinkle with half of the cheese. Repeat, ending with cheese. Bake 30 minutes. Remove and decorate edges with tortilla chips and return to oven for 10 minutes. Serves 10 to 12.

Per serving: 384 calories; 26.4 fat grams

EASY CHILE RELLENOS

Rellenos have always been a favorite of our families and friends.

1 (26-ounce) can green chiles (or 16 whole
    green chiles)
1 pound Monterey Jack cheese, cut into
    1/2-inch x 1/4-inch strips
2 cups grated cheddar cheese
5 large eggs
1/4 cup flour
1 1/4 cups milk
Salt and pepper to taste
3 dashes red pepper sauce
Paprika

Preheat oven to 400°. Spray 9x13-inch baking dish. Rinse seeds from chiles carefully. Spread chiles in single layer on paper towels and pat dry. Slip strip of Monterey Jack cheese into each chile. Beat eggs with mixer, gradually adding flour, beating until smooth. Add milk, salt, pepper and red pepper sauce. Beat well. Arrange half of the stuffed chiles in baking dish and sprinkle with half of cheese and paprika. Repeat layers ending with cheese. Pour egg mixture over all. Bake, uncovered, 30 to 40 minutes. Cut in squares. Serves 6 to 8.

Per serving: 347 calories; 23 fat grams

Make these even QUICKer by spreading chiles and 1 cup cheese into baking dish. Then pour in egg mixture topping with cheese.

QUICK CHICKEN BREAST ALA SALSA

Prepare QUICKly, put in oven, run some short errands and you'll have a scrumptious, healthy dinner when you get home.

4 chicken breasts
2 tablespoons lime juice
Salt and white pepper to taste
2 cups salsa
1 1/2 cups grated white cheddar cheese
Parmesan cheese

Preheat oven to 350°. Place chicken breasts in 9x9-inch baking dish. Sprinkle lime juice evenly over them. Salt and pepper. Pour salsa over chicken and place in oven. Bake 35 minutes or until chicken is done. Remove and spread cheeses on top. Return to oven for 5 minutes. Serve with lettuce, tomato and a mound of Spanish rice. Serves 4.

Per serving: 484 calories; 22.4 fat grams

BEEF OR CHICKEN FAJITAS

Can't you just smell those onions and peppers cooking now? Looks hard, but easy as pie. A helper to prepare the condiments will put this wonderful dinner on the table QUICKer.

1 1/2 pounds flank steak, thinly sliced, or
    chicken breasts, cut in strips
4 tablespoons oil, divided
2 tablespoons Worcestershire sauce
1/2 teaspoon chili powder
1/2 teaspoon garlic salt
1/2 teaspoon oregano
1/4 teaspoon cumin
1 large onion, sliced
1 large green pepper, cut in strips
1/2 large red pepper, cut in strips

CONDIMENTS:
1 (15-ounce) can refried beans
Salsa
Lettuce, shredded
Guacamole
Light sour cream
Tomatoes, chopped
Black Olives, sliced
Chives, chopped
8 flour tortillas, warmed

Heat beans; and put beans and other condiments on table in separate bowls. The rest of this recipe will go fast. Sauté meat in 2 tablespoons oil, Worcestershire sauce and spices over high heat in a heavy fry pan or wok. At the same time, sauté onion and peppers in 2 tablespoons oil over medium heat. Stir both to keep from scorching. Serve meat, onions and peppers on warmed plates. Have guests roll meat, onions and peppers in tortillas with chosen condiments. Serves 6.

Per serving: beef, 634 calories; 40.6 fat grams
chicken, 533 calories; 29.9 fat grams

 If you choose to grill the meat, marinate meat for a couple of hours in oil, Worcestershire sauce and spices.

You can buy packaged fajita mix, prepared guacamole, and cut up fajita meat at the grocery store.

FLAUTAS

This is a good opportunity to use leftover roast, chicken or ground beef.

2 cups beef, shredded or ground
1/2 cup chopped onion
1 (10-ounce) can enchilada sauce
1/4 cup cider vinegar
2 teaspoons chili powder
2 teaspoons oregano
1 teaspoon salt
1/4 teaspoon cumin
8 corn tortillas
1 cup shredded Monterey Jack cheese
4 tablespoons oil
Guacamole
Tomatoes
Salsa

Preheat oven to 425°. Spray 9x13-inch baking dish. In heavy skillet, brown meat; drain (or heat shredded or leftover meat). Add onion, enchilada sauce, vinegar, chili powder, oregano, salt and cumin. Simmer, uncovered, 10 minutes. Place tortillas between paper towels and heat in microwave 30 seconds. Keep tortillas warm while working. Spread 1/4 cup meat mixture along center of tortilla; top with cheese. Fold sides of tortilla over filling, rolling into flute-shape (top bigger than bottom) and place seam-side down in baking dish. Brush with cooking oil and place in oven. Bake 15 minutes. Serve with guacamole, tomatoes and salsa. Serves 4 to 6.

Per serving: 707 calories; 55.0 fat grams

BEEF TACOS

America's favorite QUICK meal.

1 1/2 pounds lean ground beef
1 medium onion, chopped
2 cloves garlic, minced
1 1/2 teaspoons chili powder
1/2 cup salsa
Salt and pepper to taste
12 taco shells

CONDIMENTS:
1 1/2 cups shredded cheddar cheese
2 medium tomatoes, chopped
1/2 medium head lettuce
Bottled taco sauce, optional

Brown ground beef in large skillet with onion, garlic, chili powder and salsa. Cook uncovered until all liquid is evaporated and meat is well browned; stir often. Add salt and pepper to taste. Spoon into taco shells and let everyone build their own with offered condiments. Serves 6.

Per serving: 546 calories; 38.9 fat grams

To make this recipe even QUICKer, use packaged taco seasoning.

CRUNCHY BAKED CHICKEN NUGGETS

4 chicken breasts
2 tablespoons lime juice
2 tablespoons honey
1 cup crushed tortilla chips
1 (15-ounce) can crushed tomatoes
1 (4-ounce) can diced green chiles
1 teaspoon granulated garlic
1/2 teaspoon salt
1/2 teaspoon oregano

Preheat oven to 400°. Spray baking sheet. Cut chicken into 1-inch strips. In large shallow dish, combine lime juice and honey. Gently stir in chicken strips, coating each one as well as possible. Place crushed chips in a clean paper bag. Drop chicken pieces into bag a few at a time and shake to coat. Place on baking sheet. Bake 10 minutes; test for doneness. Meanwhile, in medium saucepan, combine remaining ingredients. Heat to boiling and simmer 5 minutes. Spoon tomato mixture evenly on 4 plates. Lay chicken pieces on top of sauce. Garnish with cheese, lime slices and cilantro leaf. Serves 4.

Per serving: 485 calories; 17.2 fat grams

SPICY CHICKEN TACOS

A QUICK and tasty alternative to beef tacos.

4 cups shredded cooked chicken (or
    1 [10-ounce] can chunk chicken)
1 (4-ounce) can diced green chiles
1/2 cup light sour cream
1/2 teaspoon garlic salt
1/4 teaspoon oregano
1/4 teaspoon cumin
1/2 teaspoon chili powder
1 teaspoon lime juice
12 taco shells

CONDIMENTS:
1/2 head lettuce, shredded
2 medium tomatoes, chopped
2 cups grated cheddar cheese
1/2 red onion, chopped
Guacamole, optional
Pico de Gallo or salsa

Combine chicken, chiles, sour cream, garlic salt, oregano, cumin, chili powder and lime juice. Heat in microwave until hot (about 4 minutes, stirring at two minutes). Spoon into taco shells and offer condiments. Serves 6.

Per serving: 451 calories; 20.6 fat grams

 Sour cream, milk or yogurt can relieve the "fire" in the mouth.

SOFT VEGETABLE TACOS

A veggie lover's delight

1 cup grated white cheddar cheese
1 cup grated cheddar cheese
1/4 cup grated parmesan cheese
1 1/2 cups chopped broccoli
1 cup chopped cauliflower
3 carrots, sliced thin
1/2 cucumber, diced
2 cups diced zucchini
1 cup diced red pepper
1 small onion, diced
1/2 teaspoon chili powder
1/2 teaspoon garlic salt
6 flour tortillas, warmed

CONDIMENTS:
1/2 cup sliced black olives
1/2 head lettuce, shredded
2 fresh tomatoes, chopped
Guacamole, optional
Pico de Gallo

Mix cheeses together in medium mixing bowl; set aside. Steam vegetables until tender (about 10 minutes). Add chili powder and garlic salt. Spoon into warmed tortilla and spread with cheese mixture. Roll. Serve on warm plate with condiments. Serves 6.

Per serving: 355 calories; 17.8 fat grams

SOFT SEAFOOD TACOS

Cyndi first had fish tacos on the beach in Encinada, Mexico, with friends. They were deep fried in a big barrel of fat that was more than a few months old. This is Cyndi's healthier version. Don't let the length of the description scare you—they are easy!

1 pound favorite fish fillets (snapper, cod,
    trout, mahi mahi, halibut, salmon), cut
    into serving pieces
2 tablespoons butter
1 teaspoon lime juice
1/2 teaspoon hot pepper sauce
3/4 cup light sour cream
3 tablespoons skim milk
1/4 cup salsa
2 sprigs cilantro, chopped
2 green onions, chopped
Salt and pepper to taste
1 (4-ounce) can whole green chiles
4 flour tortillas
Lettuce
Tomato

Start charcoal grill. Melt butter, lime juice and pepper sauce in the microwave. Brush fish fillets with butter sauce and cook on grill until done (about 5 minutes on each side), basting with butter sauce when turned. In the meantime, mix sour cream, milk, salsa, cilantro, green onion, salt and pepper together in small bowl. Warm in microwave. Slice green chiles lengthwise to make at least 4 long pieces and warm with tortillas between moistened paper towels in microwave. When fish is done, place a piece in each of the tortillas. Place green chile on top and spread with warmed sour cream mixture, reserving 1/4 cup. Fold over. Garnish with shredded lettuce and tomato wedge. Spoon reserved sour cream mixture on top. Serves 4.

Per serving: 325 calories; 10.8 fat grams

CRISPY BURRITOS

Cyndi's daughter, Heather, created these burritos. Add any of your favorite ingredients.

4 flour tortillas
1 (15-ounce) can refried beans
1 cup shredded co-jack cheese
1/2 cup light sour cream
1/2 cup salsa

Preheat oven to 400°. Spray cookie sheet. Lay tortillas on cookie sheet. Spread even amounts of refried beans on tortillas. Layer other ingredients on top. Fold one edge of tortilla over filling, fold in both ends of tortilla and roll over seam side down. Bake 15 minutes. Serves 4.

Per serving: 319 calories; 14.3 fat grams

Serve with extra cheese, shredded lettuce, salsa and any other condiments that make your burrito complete.

RICE AND BEAN BURRITOS

An inexpensive, meatless meal.

1 tablespoon oil
2 stalks celery with leaves, sliced
2 cloves garlic, minced
1 red onion, chopped
2 (15-ounce) cans red kidney beans,
    rinsed and drained
2 cups cooked rice
1/4 cup taco sauce
1/2 teaspoon cumin
1/2 teaspoon chili powder
2 to 3 drops hot pepper sauce
4 flour tortillas, warmed

In heavy skillet, sauté celery, garlic and onion in oil until slightly tender. Mix in beans, rice and taco sauce. Add cumin, chili powder and pepper sauce. Spoon even amounts into center of tortillas. Roll and serve with salsa and salad. Serves 4.

Per serving: 475 calories; 7.6 fat grams

Leftover bacon or ham can be added to vary this recipe.

STACKED ENCHILADAS

This is one of the first recipes Cyndi used when she realized Mexican food HAD to be served two or three times a week in her home. It's been varied several ways since then.

2 cups chopped cooked chicken (or
    1 pound lean ground beef,
    browned and drained)
1 cup light sour cream
1/4 cup chopped green onions
1/2 teaspoon salt
1/4 teaspoon cumin
1 (10-ounce) can enchilada sauce (or make
    your own)
 6 corn tortillas
2 1/2 cups shredded cheddar cheese

Preheat oven to 375°. Spray 7x7x6-inch deep casserole dish. Combine meat with sour cream, onions, salt and cumin in mixing bowl. Heat enchilada sauce in medium pan. Dip 1 tortilla into enchilada sauce and place in dish. Spoon 3 to 4 tablespoons filling over tortilla. Sprinkle with 1/3 cup cheese. Repeat layers, reserving last layer of cheese. Pour remaining enchilada sauce over stack. Top with cheese and bake 30 minutes. Serves 4.

Per serving: 612 calories; 41 fat grams

 This recipe is good without the meat. Steam some vegetables to mix with the sour cream.

CHICKEN ENCHILADA CASSEROLE

M-m-m good!! Can't think of anything else to say except this makes our mouth water.

4 chicken breasts
2 chicken bouillon cubes
2 cups water
1 medium onion, minced
2 cloves garlic, minced
3 cups shredded cheddar cheese, divided
3/4 cup chicken stock (from cooking the
    chicken breasts)
1 can cream of celery soup
1 can cream of chicken soup
2 cups light sour cream
1 cup salsa
1 large package corn tortillas, cut in half

Preheat oven to 350°. Spray 9x13-inch baking dish. In saucepan, simmer chicken with bouillon cubes and water until tender. Remove from broth and set aside to cool slightly. Shred chicken or use food processor to chop chicken, onions and garlic. Mix 1 cup cheese and remaining ingredients, except tortillas, into chicken. Line bottom of dish with tortilla halves. Spread half of mixture over tortillas in baking dish. Sprinkle with 1 cup cheese. Repeat layers ending with remaining cheese. Bake 30 minutes. Serves 8.

Per serving: 686 calories; 43.6 fat grams

 Make into individual enchiladas by filling each tortilla with chicken mixture and rolling. Placing seam side down in baking dish. Top with remaining chicken mixture, grated cheese and salsa.

ENCHILADA RICE CASSEROLE

1 (14 1/2-ounce) can beef broth plus 1 cup
    water (or 2 1/2 cups hot water and
    2 beef bouillon cubes)
1 cup rice, uncooked
1 to 2 teaspoons chili powder
1 pound lean ground beef
1 onion, chopped
1 (10-ounce) can enchilada sauce (or make
    your own)
4 green onions, sliced
1 cup sliced black olives, divided
1 1/2 cups shredded Monterey Jack, Colby
    or cheddar cheese (or combination of
    all)
1 cup light sour cream
1 avocado, sliced (optional)

Preheat oven to 350°. Spray 9x9-inch baking dish. Bring beef broth to boil and stir in rice and chili powder. Lower heat, cover and simmer while browning meat and onion. Drain meat, add enchilada sauce and heat. Stir green onions into rice. Spread into baking dish. Stir 2/3 cup olives into meat mixture. Spread over rice. Top with cheese. Bake 20 minutes. Remove. Spoon sour cream down center of casserole. Arrange avocado slices and remaining olives over sour cream. Serves 6.

Per serving: 558 calories; 32.8 fat grams

This casserole can be made ahead and heated 30 to 45 minutes. If frozen, thaw (can "defrost" in microwave) before heating.

CREAMY CHICKEN CASSEROLE

1 (15-ounce) can tomato sauce
1 cup chicken broth
1 onion, chopped (divided)
1 (4-ounce) can diced green chiles
2 teaspoons salt
1/2 teaspoon cumin
1/2 teaspoon oregano
2 cups cooked chicken, cut in large pieces
3 cups rice, cooked
1 cup sour cream
2 cups shredded cheddar cheese, divided
1 1/2 cups crushed corn chips

Preheat oven to 350°. Spray 9x13-inch baking dish. Combine tomato sauce, broth, 3/4 cup onions, green chiles and seasonings. Cook over low heat 10 minutes. Add chicken. Stir together rice and sour cream. Spoon into a baking dish. Sprinkle with 1 cup cheese. Pour sauce over all. Top with remaining cheese and onions. Cover with corn chips. Bake 25 minutes. Serve with salad and more corn chips. Garnish each serving with banana pepper. Serves 6 to 8.

Per serving: 654 calories; 34.3 fat grams

WEST OF THE PECOS CASSEROLE

Cyndi's Texas friend, Harriet, shared this recipe.

6 ounces wide noodles
2 pounds lean ground beef
1 large onion
1 green pepper
1 1/2 cups celery
1 (4-ounce) can sliced mushrooms
2 teaspoons chili powder
1/4 cup Worcestershire sauce
1 (10-ounce) can tomato soup
1 (15-ounce) can cream style corn
1 (10-ounce) can tomatoes and green
    chilies
2 cups crushed tortilla chips

Preheat oven to 350°. Spray deep casserole dish. Cook noodles according to package directions. Set aside. Brown ground beef; drain. While meat is cooking, chop onion, green pepper and celery in chopper or food processor. Add to browned meat. Add remaining ingredients. Heat to simmering. Stir in cooked noodles. Pour into casserole dish. Top with crushed tortilla chips. Bake 30 minutes. Serves 8 to 10.

Per serving: 643 calories; 35.9 fat grams

 Shredded chicken or ground turkey can be substituted for the ground beef.

VEGETABLE MEXICAN LASAGNA

20 lasagna noodles, cooked according
   to package directions
1 medium zucchini, halved and thinly
   sliced
2 cloves garlic, minced (or 1 teaspoon
   garlic salt)
1 small onion, chopped
1 (15-ounce) can tomato sauce
1 (15-ounce) can red kidney beans, rinsed
   and drained
1 (10-ounce) can diced tomatoes and
   green chiles
3 cups lowfat cottage cheese
1/4 cup chopped fresh cilantro
3 cups shredded white cheddar cheese,
   divded
1 cup parmesan cheese, divided

Preheat oven to 425°. Spray 11x14-inch baking dish. Combine zucchini, garlic, onion, tomato sauce, beans, and tomatoes and green chiles in large sauce pan. Heat and simmer 10 minutes. Meanwhile, prepare filling by combining cottage cheese, cilantro, 2 cups cheddar cheese and 1/2 cup parmesan cheese. Spoon enough sauce into baking dish to cover bottom. Lay 4 to 5 lasagna noodles over sauce. Spread half of cottage cheese mixture over noodles, lay down another layer of noodles. Repeat ending with third layer of noodles and remaining sauce. Top with remaining cheddar cheese and parmesan cheese. Bake 25 minutes. Serves 10.

Per serving: 892 calories; 8.5 fat grams

 Substitute spinach or broccoli for zucchini.

BRIAN'S MEXICAN CHICKEN ENCHILADAS

Brian is Cyndi's son-in-law. He cooked this for us one night when he and Heidi were between homes; we enjoyed the leftovers for breakfast topped with an egg and salsa.

1 (10-ounce) can cream of mushroom soup
1 (10-ounce) can cream of chicken soup
1/2 cup milk
2 (4-ounce) cans diced green chiles
1/2 cup chopped onions
2 cups diced cooked chicken (or canned)
12 flour tortillas
1 pound shredded cheddar cheese
1 cup green chili salsa

Preheat oven to 400°. Spray 11x14-inch baking dish. Mix soups, milk, chiles, onion and chicken together in large saucepan and heat through. Spread enough soup mixture to cover bottom of baking dish. Top with 4 tortillas and 1/3 of cheese. Repeat 2 more times ending with cheese. Bake 30 minutes. Serves 8.

Per serving: 532 calories; 29.5 fat grams

SANDY'S ENCHILADAS

Georgie's sister, Sandy, was a bilingual/bicultural teacher in both Laredo and Dallas, Texas. This is a recipe she passed on to Georgie, and it has been a family favorite ever since.

1 pound lean ground beef
1 package chili mix
1 (15-ounce) can tomato sauce
1 (10-ounce) can enchilada sauce
1 cup water
12 corn tortillas
1 medium onion, diced
1 1/2 pounds cheddar cheese, shredded
　(divded)

Preheat oven to 350°. Spray 9x13-inch baking pan. In large pan, brown ground beef; drain. Add chili mix, tomato sauce, enchilada sauce and water. Heat until bubbly. Dip tortilla in meat mixture, covering both sides. Place 1/3 cup of cheese down center of each tortilla and sprinkle with onion to taste. Roll tortilla and place in baking pan. Repeat with remaining tortillas. Pour remaining chili mixture over tortillas and top with remaining cheese. Bake 30 minutes. Serves 6.

Per serving: 858 calories; 60.0 fat grams

SPINACH-ARTICHOKE ENCHILADAS

Meatless and yummy!

1 tablespoon butter
2 (10-ounce) packages chopped, frozen
    spinach, thawed and well drained
1 onion, diced
3 cloves garlic, minced
1/2 cup diced red pepper
1 (8 1/4-ounce) jar marinated artichoke
    hearts, drained and chopped
1 (3-ounce) package cream cheese
4 to 5 drops hot pepper sauce
Salt and pepper to taste
8 corn tortillas
8 1/4-inch strips Mozzarella cheese
1 cup light sour cream
1/2 cup light mayonnaise
1 teaspoon lime juice
1 teaspoon garlic salt
1 cup salsa

Preheat oven to 400°. Spray 9x13-inch baking dish. In large skillet, sauté butter, spinach, onion, garlic and red pepper for 5 minutes. Add artichoke hearts, cream cheese, pepper sauce, salt and pepper. Heat just until cream cheese is mixed with ingredients. Warm tortillas between damp paper towels. Spoon filling into middle of tortilla; lay cheese on top of spinach mixture and roll. Place seam side down in baking dish. In medium bowl, mix remaining ingredients. Spoon evenly over enchiladas. Bake 15 minutes. Garnish with black olives, chives and fresh tomatoes. Serves 4.

Per serving: 512 calories; 27.2 fat grams

 Add 1 cup of crab or shrimp to vary.

CHEESE QUESADILLAS

4 large flour tortillas
1/2 cup shredded cheddar cheese
1/2 cup shredded white cheddar cheese
1/2 cup shredded Monterey Jack cheese
2 tablespoons finely chopped pickled
    jalapeño peppers, (or two fresh jalape-
    ños, chopped)
1/2 cup sliced black olives, optional
Sour cream
Guacamole
Salsa

Preheat oven to 400°. Spray 2 baking sheets. Lay 2 tortillas on each sheet. In large bowl, mix cheeses together. Spread cheese equally on half of each tortilla. Spread jalapeños and olives over cheese. Fold tortilla in half. Bake 10 minutes. Garnish with a dollop of sour cream and guacamole. Offer with salsa. Serves 4.

Per serving: 281 calories; 16.1 fat grams

 For a milder quesadilla substitute diced green chiles for jalapeños.

MEAT QUESADILLAS

1/2 cup shredded cheddar cheese
1/2 cup shredded white cheddar cheese
1/2 cup shredded Monterey Jack cheese
4 large flour tortillas
2 cups cooked chicken, leftover roast beef,
    brisket or pork, shredded
1/2 cup chopped onion
1 (15-ounce) can pork green chili
Salsa

Preheat oven to 400°. In large bowl, mix cheeses together. Spray 2 baking sheets. Lay 2 tortillas on each baking sheet. Cover each tortilla with 1/2 cup meat, 1/4 cup cheese (reserve 1/2 cup cheese for top), and 1/8 cup onion. Fold tortilla over and bake 15 minutes. Meanwhile, heat green chili. Remove quesadillas from oven; spoon green chili over tortillas and top with remaining cheese. Bake 5 minutes more. Offer salsa. Serves 4.

Per serving: 816 calories; 34.7 fat grams

VEGGIE QUESADILLAS

4 large flour tortillas
1 cup shredded cheddar cheese
1 cup shredded white cheddar cheese
1/2 cup grated parmesan cheese
1 cup chopped broccoli
1 cup sliced mushrooms
1/2 cup sliced red onion
1/2 cup sliced green peppers
2 tomatoes, sliced in thin wedges
1 (15-ounce) can red or green chili

Preheat oven to 400°. Spray 2 baking sheets. Lay 2 tortillas on each baking sheet. In a small bowl, mix cheeses together. Sprinkle approximately 1/4 cup cheese mixture on half of each tortilla. Spread equal amounts of vegetables over cheese. Spoon 1 to 2 teaspoons chili over vegetables and top with remaining cheese. Fold over tortilla. Bake 15 minutes. Meanwhile, heat chili and spoon over quesadilla when served. Serves 4.

Per serving: 450 calories; 24.8 fat grams

Colorado Pork Salsa (page 36) is wonderful on this quesadilla

SUPER SIZE TOSTADAS

This tostada is a meal in itself.

1 1/2 pounds lean ground beef
1 onion, chopped
1 clove garlic, minced
1/2 cup salsa
1/4 teaspoon oregano
6 large flour tortillas
2 tablespoons butter or margarine, melted
1 (15-ounce) can refried beans
1 (15-ounce) can green chili (or use home-
    made)
2 cups shredded white cheddar cheese
2 cups shredded lettuce
Sliced black olives
Sour cream
Salsa
Chopped Green onions

Preheat oven to 400°. Brown beef in large skillet; drain. Add onion, garlic, salsa, and oregano. While meat is browning, brush tortillas lightly with butter or margarine. Bake 5 minutes, or until lightly browned and crispy. Remove from oven, cool slightly, and spread with even portions of beans, green chili, cheese and lettuce. Offer olives, sour cream, salsa and green onions for condiments. Serves 6.

Per serving: 799 calories; 51.2 fat grams

This is a great place for that extra ground beef or chicken that you prepared and froze a couple of nights ago.

STUFFED TORTILLA PIZZA

A new twist to the traditional pizza.

1 pound lean ground beef (or 2 cups cooked, shredded chicken)
1 teaspoon garlic salt
1/2 teaspoon oregano
1 1/2 cup salsa, divided
6 large flour tortillas
1 (15-ounce) can black beans, refried beans or chili beans
1 (4-ounce) can diced green chiles
3 cups shredded cheddar cheese and Monterey Jack cheese, divided

Preheat oven to 425°. Spray large baking sheet. In large skillet, brown ground beef; drain and season with garlic salt and oregano. Mix in 1/2 cup salsa. Mix beans with green chiles and spread on 2 of the tortillas. Top with 1 1/3 cups cheese. Place the other 2 tortillas on the bean mixture. Spread on another 1 1/3 cups cheese and top with meat mixture. Place the other 2 tortillas on top of meat. Spread with remaining cheese and remaining cup salsa. Bake 15 minutes. Cut into pie shaped slices and serve with favorite salad.
Serves 4 to 6.

Per serving: 783 calories; 43.4 fat grams

SKILLET PORK CHOPS 'N SALSA

The "other white meat" is tasty served with any variety of potatoes, vegetables and a tossed salad.

4 lean pork chops
1/2 teaspoon cumin
1/2 teaspoon chili powder
1/2 teaspoon garlic powder
1/2 teaspoon oregano
2 teaspoons oil
1 cup salsa
1/4 cup water
4 mild green chiles, sliced (optional)

Combine spices together in small bowl. Rub into pork chops. Brown in heavy skillet in oil, about 5 minutes on one side. Turn over and pour salsa and water over chops. Simmer, covered, on low heat about 15 minutes. Garnish with strips of green chiles laid over top of each pork chop. Serve with more salsa. Serves 4.

Per serving: 295 calories; 19.6 fat grams

The salsa is great over potatoes and rice.

MEXICAN SHEPHERDS PIE

Cyndi created this recipe with leftover stew and thought it was good enough to share.

1 cup frozen soup vegetables
2 to 3 cups leftover stew (or 1 [24-ounce] can stew)
1 (15-ounce) can chili beans
3 cups prepared instant potatoes
1/4 cup shredded white cheddar cheese
1 (4-ounce) can diced green chiles
1/4 cup grated parmesan cheese
1/2 teaspoon garlic
Salt and pepper to taste
3/4 cup shredded cheddar cheese
Salsa
Sliced green onions, optional
Sliced olives, optional

Preheat oven to 400°. Spray 9x9-inch baking dish or 4 deep-dish soup bowls. Microwave frozen vegetables 5 minutes in covered large microwaveable dish. Stir in stew and beans. Pour into prepared baking dish. In a separate bowl, add white cheese, green chiles, parmesan cheese, garlic, salt and pepper to prepared potatoes. Spoon onto stew mixture in baking dish. Sprinkle with cheddar cheese. Bake 20 minutes until hot. Garnish with salsa, sliced green onions and/or sliced olives. Serve with salad and cornbread. Serves 4.

Per serving: 520 calories; 31.4 fat grams

 Add a pinch of red pepper flakes for a little hotter flavor.

SPANISH STEAK

1 1/2 pounds round steak, 1-inch thick,
    tenderized
Salt and pepper to taste
1/2 cup flour
1/2 cup chopped onion
4 tablespoons oil
1 cup tomato juice
1 (15-ounce) can Mexican tomatoes
1/2 teaspoon chili powder
1/2 teaspoon oregano
1/2 teaspoon sage

Work salt, pepper and as much flour as possible into steak. In heavy skillet, brown onion and steak in oil. Add remaining ingredients. Simmer 1 hour, adding more tomato juice if necessary. Serves 4.

Per serving: 534 calories; 34.5 fat grams

Serve with a generous helping of rice pilaf and mexicorn.

CLASSIC TOSTADAS

Cyndi used to fry her own tortillas for tacos and tostadas, but the greasy mess got to her. Now she does it Georgie's way and buys them already prepared. Much easier and QUICKer!

1 pound lean ground beef
1 (15-ounce) can refried beans
Dash of hot pepper sauce
1 tablespoon Worcestershire sauce
1/2 teaspoon garlic powder
Salt and pepper to taste
8 flat tostada shells
1 cup shredded cheddar cheese
1 cup shredded lettuce
1 tomato, chopped
1/2 cup guacamole

In large skillet, brown ground beef; drain. Add beans, hot sauce, Worcestershire sauce, salt and pepper. Spread a thin layer of meat sauce on tostada shell; sprinkle with grated cheese. Add lettuce and tomato; top with guacamole. Serves 4.

Per serving: 641 calories; 42.9 fat grams

 If you are preparing this recipe ahead of serving time, keep meat warm in the slow cooker for as long as needed.

MEXICALI MEAT PIE

This recipe was a long-ago favorite of the Patricks. It was lost in the move to Greeley and recently found stuck between the pages of a cookbook.

6 slices bacon, microwaved on high about 5
    minutes or until crisp, break into pieces
1 pound lean ground beef
1 (8-ounce) can white corn, drained
1/4 cup finely chopped green pepper
1/4 cup finely chopped onion
1/4 cup cornmeal
1/2 teaspoon oregano
1/2 teaspoon chili powder
1 teaspoon salt
1/4 teaspoon pepper
1 (8-ounce) can tomato sauce
2 tablespoons cornmeal
1 prepared pie crust
1 egg
1/4 cup milk
1/2 teaspoon dry mustard
Salt to taste
1/2 teaspoon Worcestershire sauce
1 1/2 cups shredded cheddar cheese

Preheat oven to 425°. Spray deep dish pie plate. Brown beef; drain. Stir in corn, green pepper, onion, cornmeal, oregano, chili powder, salt, pepper and tomato sauce; simmer. Spread 2 tablespoons cornmeal on bottom of pie plate. Press pie crust into pie plate. Fill with meat mixture. Bake 25 minutes. Meanwhile, combine egg, milk, salt, mustard, Worcestershire sauce and cheese. Spread on pie. Top with bacon. Bake 5 more minutes. Serves 6.

Per serving: 685 calories; 39.4 fat grams

MEXICAN HOT DISH

1 pound ground sausage
1 large onion, chopped
1 (10-ounce) can cream of mushroom soup
1 soup can milk
1 (4-ounce) can taco sauce
1 package corn tortillas, torn into pieces
2 cups shredded cheddar cheese

Preheat oven to 400°. Spray deep dish casserole pan. In large skillet, brown sausage; drain. Add onions and cook 3 to 4 minutes. Mix in soup, milk and taco sauce. Heat to boiling. Overlap 1/2 of tortilla pieces in bottom of dish. Spoon 1/2 of meat mixture over tortillas and top with 1/2 of the cheese. Repeat the layers, ending with cheese. Bake for 30 minutes. Serve with choice of condiments and a salad. Serves 6.

Per serving: 552 calories; 47.8 fat grams

Chorizo is pork sausage highly seasoned with chili powder and garlic. Substitute in recipes for beef or pork if spicer taste is desired.

TORTILLA ROLL-UPS

Combine your favorite sandwich ingredients inside a tortilla; it is a nice alternative to bread. This particular roll-up uses leftover turkey or deli turkey and cranberry sauce.

1/2 cup canned cranberry sauce (whole or jellied)
1/4 cup mayonnaise
1 to 2 teaspoons chipotle powder
1/8 teaspoon salt, optional
4 flour tortillas
4 slices turkey
4 slices Swiss cheese
2 whole green chiles, sliced to make 4 pieces
Shredded lettuce

In small bowl, mix cranberry sauce, mayonnaise, chipotle powder and salt together. Place tortillas on serving plates. Spread equal amounts of mayonnaise mixture on tortillas. Lay turkey, cheese and chile pieces in center of tortilla. Top with lettuce. Fold one end of tortilla up, then roll tortilla around ingredients. Serves 4.

Per serving: 721 calories; 45.0 fat grams

Foot Notes

Tortilla roll-ups are good warmed, too.

Chop and mix all of these ingredients together into a salad and place inside pita bread.

BROCCOLI-GREEN CHILE STIR FRY

2 tablespoons olive oil
1 cooked chicken breast, diced
2 cups chopped broccoli
1/2 red onion, sliced and quartered
1/2 cup roasted red peppers
1 (4-ounce) can diced green chiles
4 cups fettuccini, prepared according to
    directions on package
3/4 cup chunky tomato spaghetti sauce
1/4 cup water
Parmesan cheese

In large skillet, sauté chicken, broccoli, onion, red peppers and green chiles in oil for 10 minutes. Add cooked fettuccini, spaghetti sauce and water. Cover and steam 5 minutes. Top with Parmesan cheese before serving with a salad and toasted tortillas. Serves 4.

Per serving: 581 calories; 17.3 fat grams

MINI MEXICAN MEATLOAFS

1 1/2 pounds lean ground beef
1 envelope dried onion soup mix
1 (4-ounce) can diced green chiles
1 (6-ounce) can tomato sauce
3/4 cup lowfat milk
1 egg, slightly beaten
20 to 25 soda crackers
2 tablespoons steak sauce

Preheat oven to 400°. Spray muffin tin cups. In large bowl, mix all ingredients thoroughly. Scoop about 1/3 cup beef mixture into each of the 12 muffin cups; press down lightly. Garnish with a drop of ketchup and a slice of green chile. Bake 20 minutes. Serves 6.

Per serving: 410 calories; 26.3 fat grams

Make the meat mixture into meatballs and cook with your favorite soup, or use it to stuff a green pepper.

GRILLED CHICKEN SANDWICH

4 chicken breast halves, slightly flattened
1 teaspoon chili powder
1 teaspoon garlic powder
1/2 teaspoon dried onion flakes
1/4 teaspoon salt
1/4 teaspoon pepper
1/2 cup light mayonnaise
1/4 cup salsa
1/4 teaspoon lime juice
4 hamburger buns
4 strips green chile
4 slices white cheddar cheese
1/2 cup guacamole
1 cup shredded lettuce
1 tomato, sliced

Start grill. Mix chili powder, garlic powder, onion flake, salt and pepper together in small bowl. Rub mixture evenly into chicken breasts. Place chicken breasts on grill and cook about 10 minutes, turning over after 5 minutes. Cut in thickest part to test doneness. In a small bowl, mix mayonnaise, salsa and lime juice. Warm buns either in microwave or on grill. Prepare remaining ingredients, either by placing on bun or by offering in separate dishes. Serves 4.

Per serving: 664 calories; 42.8 fat grams

CHILI CHEESEBURGER

This can be one of the QUICKest meals you fix and a great way to use leftover chili.

1 1/2 pounds lean ground beef made into 4
    patties
1 package taco seasoning mix
4 cups leftover chili (or canned)
1 cup shredded cheddar cheese
1 onion, diced
4 hamburger buns

Start grill. Sprinkle 1 tablespoon taco seasoning on top of each hamburger patty. Place on grill. Cook 5 to 7 minutes each side, depending on desired doneness. Lay each on bottom half of buns and top with chili, cheese and onion. Serves 4.

Per serving: 988 calories; 60.9 fat grams

The hamburger patties can also be pan fried. Canned green chili can be substituted for red chili.

Notes:

Desserts

CINNAMON TRIANGLES

Quick and delicious!

4 flour tortillas (small)
4 tablespoons butter, melted
1/2 cup sugar
1 teaspoon cinnamon
Dash of cloves

Preheat oven to 400°. Cut each tortilla into four triangles then place triangles on cookie sheets. Brush with melted butter and bake in oven 5 minutes. Remove from oven, turn, brush with butter, and bake another 5 minutes (watching carefully so they don't burn). Remove from oven and sprinkle with a mixture of sugar and spices. Serves 4.

Per serving: 313 calories; 13.9 fat grams

 Serve alone, with a meal, or tucked around dips of ice cream drizzled with caramel topping and sprinkled with a little cinnamon sugar (or try Kahlua instead of caramel). M-m-m.

SOPAIPILLAS

These are easy, messy, and lots of fun to make.

4 cups oil
2 cups flour
1 teaspoon baking powder
1 teaspoon salt
3/4 cup water

Mix dry ingredients. Add water and mix. The dough will be stiff. Let set 10 minutes. Heat oil on low while preparing dough. Divide the dough in half and roll out on floured surface to 1/8- to 1/4-inch thickness. Cut into 4x4-inch pieces. Repeat with other half of dough. Drop into hot oil. Brown on one side, turn with slotted spoon and brown on other side. Drain on layers of paper towels. Serve with honey or stuffed with vanilla ice cream. Serves 8.

Per serving: 234 calories; 13.9 fat grams

 Use this dough for empanadas, too.

MINI CHOCO-TACOS

This recipe was given to us by our friend, Renata. It sounds complicated but is really easy to make. For fancier tacos squeeze whipped topping through a decorator bag.

24 mini taco shells
2 cups semisweet chocolate chips, divided
1/3 cup butter or margarine
1 tablespoon plus 1/4 cup milk, divided
1 cup finely chopped pecans or walnuts
12 maraschino cherries, halved
3/4 cup semisweet chocolate chips
1/2 teaspoon rum or vanilla extract (can use Kahlua or Amaretto)
2/3 cup marshmallow cream
2 cups whipped topping (can use 1 cup real cream, whipped)
2 tablespoons powdered sugar

Preheat oven to 350°. Lay taco shells on a cookie sheet and bake 6 minutes. Remove and cool. In a shallow dish, melt 1 1/4 cups chocolate chips and butter in microwave, stirring after each minute until chocolate is melted. Stir in 1 tablespoon milk. Spread nuts on sheet of waxed paper. Dip outer surface of shells one at a time in chocolate mixture and lay on nuts covering outer sides. Chill 1 to 2 hours or until chocolate is hardened. In large bowl, melt 3/4 cup chocolate chips and 1/4 cup milk in microwave, stirring every minute until chocolate is melted. Remove and stir in extract. Add marshmallow cream. Refrigerate to cool. Mix whipped topping and powdered sugar. Reserve 1/2 cup for garnish and fold rest into chocolate mixture. Spoon 2 to 3 tablespoons filling into taco shells. Freeze 1 to 2 hours. Just before serving, spoon reserved whipped topping evenly onto each taco. Top with cherry half. Makes 24. Serves 12.

Per serving: 346 calories; 9.1 fat grams

MEXICAN WEDDING CAKES

These little cookies are scrumptious and favorites of ours since childhood.

1 cup butter, softened
1/2 cup powdered sugar
1 teaspoon vanilla
2 1/4 cups flour
1/2 teaspoon salt
1 cup finely chopped pecans
Powdered sugar for coating

Preheat oven to 400°. Cream butter, sugar and vanilla together in large mixing bowl. Blend flour, salt and pecans into butter and sugar mixture. Mix dough until it holds together. Form into 1-inch balls. Place balls on ungreased baking sheet, about 1 inch apart. Bake 10 to 12 minutes or until lightly browned (watch closely). Cool cookies for a few minutes and roll in powdered sugar several times until well coated. Makes 4 dozen.

Per serving: 70 calories; 4.6 fat grams

DESSERT EMPANADAS

These little "pies" are easy to take on picnics or to buffets.

1 1/2 cups flour
1/2 teaspoon salt
1/2 teaspoon sugar
1 teaspoon baking powder
1/4 teaspoon allspice
1/2 cup butter, cut into small pieces
3 egg yolks
1/3 cup milk
1 (21-ounce) can pie filling of choice
    (lemon, blueberry, cherry, apple)
3 teaspoons butter, melted

Preheat oven to 375°. Combine flour, salt, sugar, baking powder and allspice in large mixing bowl. Add butter and cut into flour with fork or pastry blender. Beat egg yolks until light and combine with milk. Stir into flour mixture to form soft dough. Roll out on floured board and cut into 3-inch circles (use drinking glass if you don't have a cookie cutter that big). Spoon 2 teaspoons pie filling into center. Moisten edges slightly with water and fold over filling. Press together with fork tongs. Brush with melted butter and bake 15 minutes. Makes about 48.

Per serving: 51 calories; 2.6 fat grams

 To make this QUICKer, use prepared pie crust.

PUMPKIN EMPANADAS

Use same crust recipe as in dessert empanadas, or use prepared pie crust.

1 cup pumpkin
1/2 cup raisins, optional
1/2 teaspoon anise
2 teaspoons cinnamon
1 teaspoon allspice
1/4 cup sugar
Pie dough
3 to 4 teaspoons butter, melted

Preheat oven to 425°. Spray cookie sheets. Combine all ingredients, except pie crust and melted butter, in saucepan. Bring to boil and simmer 10 minutes. Roll out dough and cut into 1 1/2- to 2-inch circles. Spoon 1 teaspoon filling on circle and moisten slightly with water. Cover with another circle and seal with fork tongs. Prick tops of each. Brush with butter and bake 20 minutes. Sprinkle with cinnamon sugar if desired. Serves 8 to 10

Per serving: 207 calories; 10.8 fat grams

FIESTA HOT CHOCOLATE

Chocolate dates back to the 16th Century Aztec empire, when cocoa beans were used as currency. Cyndi can relate to this love of chocolate.

6 cups milk
1/2 teaspoon cinnamon
2 teaspoons vanilla
1 1/2 cups unsweetened chocolate chips
1/4 cup sugar
2 egg yolks, beaten
Cinnamon sticks

Combine milk, cinnamon and vanilla in saucepan. Heat to almost boiling. Add chocolate and sugar; stir until melted. Slowly add the egg yolks, mixing rapidly so they don't curdle. Pour into mugs and garnish with cinnamon sticks. More sugar may be offered if not sweet enough for your guests.
Serves 6.

Per serving: 413 calories; 22.3 fat grams

BAKED APPLE FLAUTAS

Georgie doesn't like cooked apples, but found, along with the rest of her family, these apple flautas a tasty treat.

1 (21-ounce) can apple pie filling
6 small flour tortillas
4 tablespoons butter, melted
1/2 teaspoon cinnamon
1 tablespoon sugar

Preheat oven to 350°. Spray baking sheet. Place 1/4-cup filling down center of each tortilla, avoiding edges. Roll each and pinch ends together. If ends don't seal, moisten inside edges with water and try again. Brush each tortilla roll with butter. Place on baking sheet, seam side down. Mix cinnamon and sugar; sprinkle over tortillas. Bake 10 minutes. Serve hot either by themselves or with vanilla ice cream. Serves 6.

Per serving; 290 calories; 10.2 fat grams

 Try with cherry or blueberry filling.

STRAWBERRY-MARGARITA PIE

QUICK and refreshing after a heavy, spicy Mexican dinner.

1 (9-inch) prepared graham cracker pie
    crust
1 (10-ounce) package frozen strawberries in
    syrup, thawed
1 (8-ounce) package cream cheese, softened
1/2 cup frozen strawberry margarita mix,
    thawed
1 (4-ounce) container light whipped topping

Whirl strawberries, cream cheese and margarita mix in blender until smooth. In large bowl, mix strawberry mixture with whipped topping. Pour into pie crust. Freeze 4 to 6 hours. Garnish with fresh strawberries and lime slices. Serves 10.

Per serving: 255 calories; 17.4 fat grams

BREAD PUDDING WITH KAHLUA CREAM

Most of us don't think of bread pudding as a Mexican dessert; traditionally it is made with a special brown sugar sauce that is alleged to be sweeter and more flavorful than our brown sugar.

10 slices bread, broken in pieces
1/2 cup raisins, optional
4 eggs, well beaten (or 1 cup egg substitute)
2 cups milk
1 teaspoon vanilla
1/2 cup brown sugar
1/2 teaspoon nutmeg
1 teaspoon cinnamon
1/4 teaspoon cloves
1 1/2 cups light whipped topping
1/4 cup Kahlua (add more if preferred)

Preheat oven to 400°. Spray 9x13-inch baking dish. In large bowl, place bread and raisins. In a separate bowl, beat eggs, milk, vanilla, sugar and spices. Gently stir into bread pieces. Pour into baking dish. Sprinkle with additional cinnamon and nutmeg if desired. Set inside a slightly bigger baking dish filled with hot water. Bake 50 to 60 minutes. Add Kahlua to whipped topping container. Serve Bread Pudding warm with Kahlua Cream. Serves 8.

Per serving: 305.5 calories; 11.8 fat grams

Notes:

Index

Quick Crockery Cooking
$12.95 • 168 pages

Quick Desserts
$12.95 • 168 pages

Quick Hors d'oeuvres
$12.95 • 168 pages

Quick Lunches & Brunches
$12.95 • 168 pages

Quick Mexican Cooking
$12.95 • 168 pages

Quick Soups 'n Salads
$12.95 • 168 pages

Great American Cookbooks

Call TOLL-FREE **1-866-625-9241**
to order or request free information about our cookbooks

Visit us ONLINE at **www.greatamericanpublishers.com**
• Convenient online ordering
• Free Recipes
• Fundraising opportunities
• Information about getting your book published

- -

Order Form MAIL TO: Great American Publishers • P. O. Box 1305 • Kosciusko, MS 39090

❑ Check Enclosed

Charge to: ❑ Visa   ❑ MC   ❑ AmEx   ❑ Disc

Card#_____

Exp Date_____ Signature_____

Name_____

Address_____

City_____ State_____ Zip_____

Phone_____

Email_____

Qty.	Title	Total
____	**Quick Crockery Cooking** $12.95 each	_____
____	**Quick Desserts** $12.95 each	_____
____	**Quick Hors d'oeuvres** $12.95 each	_____
____	**Quick Lunches & Brunches** $12.95 ea.	_____
____	**Quick Mexican Cooking** $12.95 each	_____
____	**Quick Soups 'n Salads** $12.95 each	_____

Subtotal _____

Postage ($3 1st book; $.50 each additional) _____

Total _____